9/6

# Documents on British
# Economic and Social History
# Book II    1870–1939

## THE DECLINE AND FALL OF BRITISH
## ECONOMIC SUPREMACY

DOCUMENTS ON BRITISH
ECONOMIC AND SOCIAL HISTORY

Book One 1750–1870
Book Two 1870–1939
Book Three 1945–67

*The aim of these books is to provide pupils in secondary schools with a full survey of the developments in British economic and social life since 1750.*

# Documents on British Economic and Social History

Book Two 1870–1939

## PETER LANE

HEAD OF THE HISTORY DEPARTMENT
COLOMA COLLEGE, WEST WICKHAM, KENT

MACMILLAN
London · Melbourne · Toronto
1968

# ACKNOWLEDGEMENTS

The editor and publishers would like to thank the following, who have kindly given permission for the use of copyright material: George Allen & Unwin Ltd., for the extract from *The Glory of Parliament*, by H. Boardman; Associated Newspapers Ltd., for the letter from *Sweated Industries*, a handbook of the *Daily News* Exhibition 1906; The Bodley Head, for extracts from *Life's Enchanted Cup*, by Mrs. C. S. Peel; Miss Sonia Brownell and Secker & Warburg Ltd., for the extract from *The Road to Wigan Pier*, by George Orwell; Cave, Drake, Sturton & Co., for the extract from *Industrial Democracy*, by Sidney and Beatrice Webb; Mr. Robert Graves and Mr. Alan Hodge, Faber & Faber Ltd., and Collins-Knowlton-Wing Inc., for extracts from *The Long Weekend*; Longmans, Green & Co. Ltd., for the extract from *British Industries and Their Organisation*, by Professor G. C. Allen; Macdonald & Co. (Publishers) Ltd., for the extract from *Let Candles Be Brought In*, by Sir Geoffrey Shakespeare; Frederick Muller Ltd. and Frank C. Betts Ltd., for the extract from *Neville Chamberlain*, by Iain Macleod; Thomas Nelson & Sons Ltd., for the extracts from *Poverty: A Study in Town Life*, by B. Seebohm Rowntree; Mr. Arthur Pratt, for the extract from *An Autobiography*, by Viscount Snowden; The Public Trustee and The Society of Authors, for the extract from *Fortnightly Review*, 1st November 1893, by George Bernard Shaw; Lord Salter, for extracts from *Memoirs of a Public Servant*; Mrs. Mary Stocks, for the extract from *Eleanor Rathbone*; *The Times*, for 'The Workpeople's Polytechnic', 'Joseph Chamberlain's Tariff Reform Campaign, 20th January 1904', and 'The Dockers' Strike, 1889'; and the *Yorkshire Evening Post*, for the extract on the opening of Quarry Hill flats from the issue of 30th March 1938.

The editor and publishers wish to state that they have occasionally slightly adapted the language of the more obscure documents to help the modern reader, but they have been scrupulously anxious not to distort the original meaning of the document.
The questions sometimes need more knowledge than the documents alone can give. It is hoped that this will encourage research.
The author wishes to thank Mr. W. J. Fowler for his helpful suggestions.

© Peter Lane 1968
*Published by*
MACMILLAN AND CO LTD
*Little Essex Street London* W C 2
*and also at Bombay Calcutta and Madras*
*Macmillan South Africa (Publishers) Pty Ltd Johannesburg*
*The Macmillan Company of Australia Pty Ltd Melbourne*
*The Macmillan Company of Canada Ltd Toronto*

Printed in Great Britain by Richard Clay (The Chaucer Press) Ltd, Bungay, Suffolk

# Contents

## ACKNOWLEDGEMENTS FOR ILLUSTRATIONS

The publishers wish to thank the following for kind permission to reproduce the illustrations on the pages quoted: Aerofilms: 38 (lower); British Motor Corporation: 18 (upper); Greater London Council: 28 (lower), 38 (upper), 118 (all); Imperial Chemical Industries: 18 (lower); Illustrated London News: 28 (upper), 88 (upper); Keystone Press Agency: 68 (upper); National Coal Board: 55; National Society for the Prevention of Cruelty to Children: 41; Punch: 48 (upper), 108 (both); Radio Times Hulton Picture Library: 47, 58 (all), 63, 77, 78 (both), 88 (lower), 98 (both), 117, 121, 127.

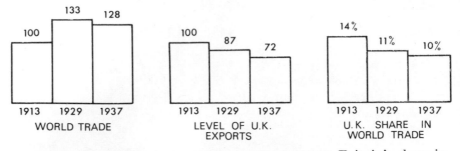

1a. While world trade increased from 1913 to 1937, Britain's share in this trade declined.

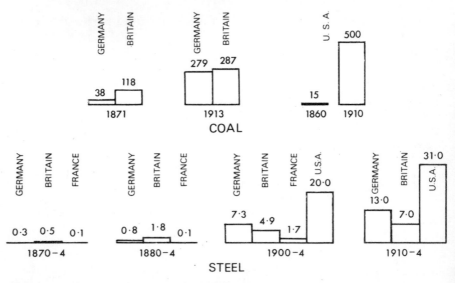

1b. Average annual output in million tons.

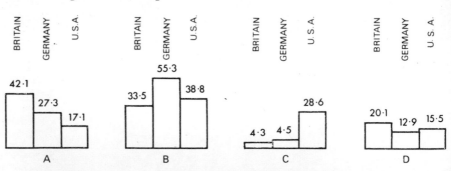

1c. Exports of manufactured goods 1913–29.

A comparison of Great Britain's, Germany's and the United States' share in the world trade of manufactured goods 1913–29. The table is divided into group A, where the world growth of trade increased by less than 75% during the period 1913–29, group B, where the world growth of trade expanded by 75–150%, group C, where it expanded by more than 150%, and group D, where there is no knowledge of the rate of expansion.

# Comment

Britain had been the world's leading industrial power in 1870, the first country to have an Industrial Revolution and to undertake massive railway building. By the end of the century Germany and the U.S.A. were rivals to Britain; in some industries they had outstripped her (Plate 1b).

In the period 1870–1939 there were rapid-growth industries (cars and chemicals), medium-growth industries (steel) and industries with a slow rate of growth (cotton and coal). As Plate 1c shows, Britain had most of her trade (and most of her investment) in the industries which were expanding least. The U.S.A. had most of hers in industries which were developing rapidly.

The effect of this can be seen in Plate 1a. Britain's share of world trade fell from 1913 to 1937; Britain's level of exports also fell. Other countries had become more efficient workshops. One result of this was unemployment.

# Questions

a. The car industry (Document 6) and the chemical industry (Document 5) were industries which were growing rapidly. What evidence is there that Britain's share in such industries was lower than that of the U.S.A. and Germany?

b. The coal industry (Document 7) and cotton industry (Document 8) were industries which were not growing so rapidly. What evidence is there that Britain had most of her investment in such industries?

c. Compare the volume of world trade in 1913, 1929 and 1937. What had happened to Britain's share in this trade?

d. What happened to the level of British exports in the period 1913–37? What effect would this have on employment in industries dependent on the export trade?

e. Read Documents 2 and 3. How do the figures in Plate 1b show that American and German industrialists invested more heavily in the steel industry than did the British industrialist?

# 1 The Depression in Agriculture, 1882

There is agreement as to the extent of the distress which has fallen upon the agricultural community. Owners and occupiers have alike suffered from it. All without distinction have been involved in a general calamity.

The two most prominent causes are bad seasons and foreign competition, aggravated by the increased cost of production and the heavy losses of livestock.

Formerly the farmer, affected by an unprecedented succession of bad seasons, was compensated by a higher price for a smaller yield; he has had in recent years to compete with an unusually large supply at greatly reduced prices.

On the other hand, he has had the advantage of an extended supply of feeding stuffs, such as Indian corn, linseed and cotton cakes and of artificial manures imported from abroad. The witnesses who speak in the interests of agriculture fully recognise the advantage to the community that food should be cheap.

*Agricultural Labour*

Labour has been more costly, so that the average labour bill of an arable farm is at least 25 per cent higher than it was some 20 years ago; from the competition of other industries the labouring class has been scarcely, if at all, affected by the distress which has fallen so heavily upon owners as well as occupiers. Provisions have been cheap and employment abundant, while wages in a few districts only have been slightly reduced.

*Report from H.M. Commissioners on Agriculture, 1882.*

# Comment

The Government set up a Commission in 1879 to examine the condition of the industry, which was asking for protection. Successive Governments, wedded to the ideas of Free Trade, refused to give the industry the protection it asked for; prices continued to fall — by 1897 wheat prices were 50% below the level of 1877, beef prices had fallen by 40%, wool by 50%, potatoes by 30%. The Americans, Australian and Argentinian farmers were helped by internal railway development (often built by British firms, financed by British capital), and improved steam-shipping (in which Britain led the world).

# Questions

a. Who was involved in 'a general calamity'?
b. What four 'prominent causes' are given to explain the depression?
c. What had happened to prices 'in recent years'? How had this affected the British farmer?
d. What evidence is there that there had been bad harvests for an unusually long period? How had bad harvests affected prices in the past?
e. What benefits had farmers gained from cheaper imports? Can you say whether this helped the dairy farmer or the arable farmer?
f. How had the farm workers been affected by the depression? (Wages, other forms of employment, prices.)
g. '. . . and foreign competition'. Show that overseas railway development and the growth of steam-shipping affected the British farmer.
h. Name three countries which supplied Britain with: (i) wheat; (ii) beef; (iii) mutton. Why had they not exported to Britain until 'recent years'?

# 2 The Decline in the Iron and Steel Trades, 1900

British manufacturers had a monopoly of the home market and foreign countries, as yet undeveloped, and no competition in British Colonies. The methods of production, first established in the United Kingdom, have since 1870 extended to foreign countries; and these countries have encouraged national industries similar to those carried on here; thus foreign manufacturers have obtained growing home markets, from which British products have been shut out by import duties. In recent years their policy has been directed to the capture of the home, foreign and colonial trade of the United Kingdom. By attacking our home market, which is open to them without let or hindrance, they have diminished the competitive power of British manufacturers in neutral markets, and they are now threatening our position in British Colonies.

Manufacturers in this country are blamed because they do not show greater enterprise in laying down large capacity plants, such as are common in the United States and in Germany. Some American furnaces, with complete equipment, cost over £200,000 each, whereas the average cost of British furnaces is not probably over £25,000.

English engineers, on visiting American workshops, have been surprised to see so few men about. Automatic machinery is much more largely used there than in this country. The combination of up-to-date plants, economies, and improvements has enabled our American rivals, paying the highest wages known in the trade, to produce plates at a cost of only about 3s. 6d. per ton for labour, averaging some 225 tons of plates per shift. These results are not equalled in our own mills.

*Report of the Tariff Commission*, 1904.

# Comment

This is an extract from the Report of the Tariff Commission, 1904, an unofficial body formed in support of Joseph Chamberlain's Tariff Reform Campaign. Chamberlain was unsuccessful in this campaign; he was supported by only part of the Tory Party, and rejected completely by the Free Trade Liberals who won the Election of 1905–6.

Chamberlain advocated Tariff Reform (Document 38) for a number of reasons, e.g. to help British industry face foreign competition and to unite the Empire by Imperial Preference. He intended to use the money collected by the tariff for the creation of a welfare state with old-age pensions, unemployment benefits, etc.

# Questions

a. In what three different markets did British iron manufacturers have 'a monopoly' in the past?
b. Why had this monopoly been lost?
c. What is an import duty? How would it affect the demand for British iron in a foreign country?
d. Why was the British market 'open without let or hindrance'?
e. How had this affected the 'competitive power' of British firms?
f. What was the average cost of: (i) a British furnace; (ii) an American furnace?
g. Why were 'so few men about' in American workshops? How did this affect the price of plates produced in their ironworks?
h. What evidence is given in Documents 1 and 2 to suggest that 1870 is 'a turning point' in British economic history?

# 3 The Failure of the British Educational System

A. I saw the wonderful Creusot exhibit, that of the firm where all the Boer guns were made. It is an example of extensive and complete organization of engineering factory methods — where one proprietor gives employment to tens of thousands of men, and produces not only a great variety of engineering products, but some of them of gigantic size; bridges, cannon, engines, dynamos and the metals from which these are all made. The Krupp exhibit is like the Creusot one in its scope and the scale of the work it represents. America is not behind-hand in this kind of elaborate and widespread factory organization. Beside Krupps, England presents a sorry spectacle. Here and there you see something English; but one is struck by the fewness of English exhibits and the general want of 'go' they indicate. I walked through the French department, devoted to the illustration of the educational and research work done by the Government in furtherance of scientific knowledge bearing on agriculture and its improvement.

B. There is a change for the better, but it did not come till long after it was an urgent necessity, and it has not yet gone nearly far enough. We see one of the evil consequences of our educational deficiencies in the much less rapid progress that we have made in those branches of industry which are the outcome of the scientific discoveries of recent times. These depend on original research, and on the intelligent appreciation, by the capitalist and commercial class, of the resources of science and the advantages of scientific training and scientific work as forces in promoting industrial progress.

Mary and Kenneth Swan, *Sir Joseph Wilson Swan — a Memoir*, 1929.

# Comment

The author of these extracts, Joseph Swan, had played a large part in the formation of the electric lamp industry, and is here giving (A) his impression of the Paris Exhibition of 1900 and (B) a lecture to students of the school of pharmacy in London in 1903.

British industrialists had created an industrial revolution by 'rule-of-thumb' methods, by trial and error (see Abraham Darby, Book I, Document 7). Their successors, impressed by the accomplishments of the older men, and themselves the products of the education of the factory, were unwilling to believe that schooling and university training were required by leaders of industry. Workmen 'learned by doing' and not by higher education. (See Documents 45 and 47.)

# Questions

a. How does this document show that Creusot works were: (i) large; (ii) producing a variety of products?
b. How did Krupps (Germany) and America compare with this?
c. How did British exhibits compare with others?
d. How had things changed by 1903? Was Joseph Swan content in 1903?
e. Why was Britain lagging behind in the new industries?
f. Why did new industries require higher education for: (i) research workers; (ii) investors; (iii) workers?
g. How does this document help us to understand the British failure to develop British inventions? (Use a modern example such as the jet air-engine or swing-wing aircraft.)
h. When were technical schools established in Britain? (See Documents 45-7.)

# 4 Montagu Norman and the Gold Standard

He was, above all, not moved by science or economics, despising the views of industrialists, trade unionists and economists, neither ready nor able, as he showed in his evidence before the Macmillan Committee on Finance and Industry, to explain his actions.

Throughout these decisive years, British monetary policy was treated as the personal prerogative of a man prepared to sacrifice the economic interests of Britain for those of the City.

On 7th July 1923, the Bank Rate was raised from three per cent to four per cent despite a Treasury warning that such a rise might have serious effects on employment. It was, said Keynes, 'one of the most misguided movements that ever occurred'; for prices were falling and unemployment severe and this was bound to worsen the situation. But it was a necessary first stage in Norman's campaign for a return to gold.

Nearly two years, and a rise in the Bank Rate to five per cent were needed to achieve his objective. But in April 1925 he could claim success. Britain returned to the gold standard at the prewar parity, thereby pricing many of her exports, including coal, out of export markets, provoking an attack on wages over a wide front, and precipitating first a coal strike and then the General Strike.

Yet it was all illusion. The international confidence, for which the temporary distresses of industry were a price to pay, was blown apart by the gales that swept the world but whose cause and strength he so resolutely refused to recognize.

Francis Williams, *A Pattern of Rulers*, 1965.

# Comment

Montagu Norman was the Governor of the Bank of England from April 1920 until January 1944; its profit, and the profit of other members of the City of London (clients of the Bank), was greatest when London was the world's financial centre (Document 37) with the £ regarded as the 'safest' currency. Norman wanted to restore the £ to its pre-war position because he thought that this was an essential part of London's claim to be the financial centre. Restoring the £ meant increasing export prices as the following figures show. (Documents 7 and 32 also.)

Assume that the price of a British car is £200.
If the exchange rate is $4.02 to £, price in U.S.A. = $804;
$4.80 to £, price in U.S.A. = $960.

# Questions

a. Whose views did Montagu Norman 'despise'?
b. What power had he during the 'decisive years' of the 1920s?
c. What did (i) the Treasury, (ii) Keynes, think about the rise in the Bank Rate in July 1923?
d. What level did Bank Rate reach in April 1925? What was Norman's 'objective'?
e. How did Britain's return to the Gold Standard affect (i) the price of coal export; (ii) the amount of coal exported?
f. Coal was priced 'out of export markets'. Why would coal owners want a reduction in miners' wages? How did the miners react to this?
g. How successful was Montagu Norman in his attempt to create a 'magnificent edifice'? Why is 1931 an important date in this respect?
h. Why did Montagu Norman want a higher Bank Rate? Was his policy successful?

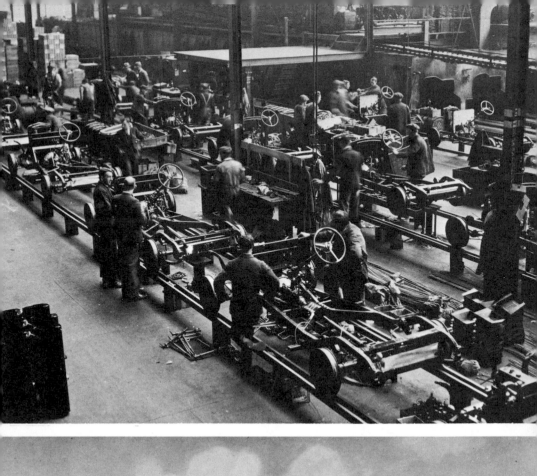

# Comment

In such a line the workmen stay at one place; the work is brought to them. Every part of making the car has been very carefully considered, and machines have been designed to do many of the processes. Each workman performs only one part of the manufacturing process. Constant repetition means that he does this part more skilfully than if he were trying to do many jobs.

By this 'mass production' system goods are produced more cheaply (see Documents 6, 10 and 11). It meant increased employment for the workpeople and for those connected with servicing and maintaining the product (see Document 6).

The car industry did not use coal, but electricity (Document 7). This meant a cleaner industry and industrial area, and less danger of industrial diseases (Document 19).

# Questions

a. Name three of the things in this moving assembly line on which a manufacturer would have to spend money (invest) before he could start producing. Why might this lead to the formation of a company? (See Document 5.)

b. This assembly line moves at about 10 feet per minute. Why could a workman do only a small part of the process of making the car? Why should this mean a better-quality car than if each man tried to do the whole job?

c. Each man did a particular job. Why could this happen only if a large number of cars were produced?

d. If a large number of cars are produced, they have to be sold. Why did this require; (i) a lowering of price; (ii) attention to selling and servicing? (See Document 6.)

e. Why is there less smoke here than in the older industries?

2a. The main assembly line at the Cowley factory near Oxford.

2b. Brunner and Mond's chemical works at Winnington, Cheshire, in 1873.

# 5 The Birth of Imperial Chemical Industries

I was in the service of John Hutchinson & Co. as head of the works office. I do not know any details of Mond's negotiations with Hutchinson, nor even what royalty was agreed on; but I understood that Hutchinson paid him about £10,000. Mond was an earnest worker, occupied in putting his process into shape at Hutchinson's works.

He and I, discussing our future, came to the conclusion that we would try working together, as manufacturers.

Mond came to me one evening to say that he had heard of Ernest Solvay's success in the conversion of salt into carbonate of soda at his works at Couillet in Belgium.

It was agreed that Mond should see Solvay with a view to taking a licence from him. Mond returned to England to tell me that he thought Solvay was at the beginning of a big success.

When we had decided to adopt the Solvay process, Mond and I went from Widnes to Hartford to choose a site upon which to establish our works.

After further investigation of the salt field of Cheshire, we hit upon the land at Winnington as being the most suitable for our purpose. It had a long frontage to the River Weaver and easy access by water to the Liverpool docks, and it had railway connection with the Cheshire Lines.

We borrowed through Messrs. Parker, Rooke and Parker, solicitors, £12,000. We mortgaged all but the works land and we paid them off on the formation of a limited company in March 1881.

John Watts, *The first 50 years of Brunner, Mond and Co., 1873–1923.*

# Comment

Alfred Mond, a scientist trained in Germany, emigrated to this country in 1862 and joined the firm of John Hutchinson and Co. at Widnes in Lancashire (paragraph 1). Here he exploited the process which he had patented for extracting sulphur from alkali waste. He later became interested in a new process discovered by a Belgian (Ernest Solvay). This was a cheap method of getting soda from salt (paragraph 3).

Mond needed the co-operation of the trained accountant, such as Brunner, to administer an office, advise him on finance and help him on the non-industrial side. Brunner would require a staff for this — and here we have the emergence of a new middle class of accountants, clerks, office managers and the like. All this work was suitable for women — and their chances of getting work increased with the technological revolution. (See Document 9.)

The new firm grew and in 1926 became Imperial Chemical Industries.

# Questions

a. Who was the author of the extract? What was his position?
b. What is a royalty? Why would Hutchinson have paid Mond 'about £10,000'?
c. What was Solvay's process? Where had this been developed?
d. What did Mond: (i) think about this process; (ii) do about it?
e. Where did they go to choose a site?
f. Why did they want: (i) to be near the salt field; (ii) to have access to the river?
g. How did Mond and Brunner: (i) obtain enough money to begin their partnership; (ii) pay off their original loan?
h. How does the document show: (i) the need for a more educated staff; (ii) increased opportunities for women? (Think of science and Document 3; office staff in large companies, Document 9.)

# 6 William Morris Explains His Success, February 1924

The success of Morris Motors happened because we took the steps to achieve a continually improving product, a reduction of cost so that prices could fall. The best way was to get specialists on every separate unit of the job. The work is better and more cheaply done. Even at the present moment, we have contracts running with at least 200 firms for various parts. At Oxford we merely assemble.

The firm that makes only one important part is probably making larger quantities than we should. It is interested in nothing else; it can keep its brains on that unit. We frequently ask contracting firms to do work at prices that they believe to be impossibly low. Usually they have not realised the savings of standardising operations [Plate 2], a continual flow of work.

Until the worker goes to his factory by car, I shall not believe that we have touched more than the fringe of the home market. The dealer has got into the habit of thinking of car sales in small numbers. Our aim is to sell cars in large numbers [Plate 3b]. For instance, if one of our dealers sold a hundred cars last year we want a sale of 200 cars next year.

One anxiety is the cost of repairs. A little garage in Cornwall may charge three times as much as a city garage. We are instituting a system of standardised repair charges. One of the things we have to impress on the dealer is the necessity for holding a sufficient stock of spare parts, to give service to owners of Morris cars. The satisfied owner is one of the best selling media in this trade — for motorists are talkers of 'shop'. By service you can keep the owner satisfied — and get his selling force behind your product.

Andrews and Brunner, *Life of Lord Nuffield*, 1955.

# Comment

The internal-combustion engine was developed in Europe in the 1880s by Daimler and Benz. In the 1890s several British firms began to build motor-cars. These firms were often the offshoots of cycle firms (Document 10) and they treated the building of a car as a craft. None of them used mass-production methods at first: they were content to build a few cars for the wealthy.

The American firms, particularly Ford's, had a different aim. They wanted to provide a cheap car. To provide such a car they used 'assembly-line' methods of production, i.e. the car was not built by a number of craftsmen but by semi-skilled machine workers. Each of these did one or two jobs to each 'body' as it came past him on an assembly line. This large-scale method of production meant that a large number of cars were produced cheaply (see reference to large factories in Document 2).

William Morris and Herbert Austin were the first to try to produce a cheap British car. Morris explained his success in this extract.

# Questions

a. Why did Morris try to reduce his costs? How would this affect the sale of his cars?
b. How many firms made parts for the Morris Company? Why is the car industry called an 'assembly industry'?
c. Why, according to Morris, would (say) Lucas make a better, cheaper battery than Morris himself?
d. Why would such a firm welcome a continual order from Morris?
e. What proportion of the population were car-owners at the time? How would (i) prices, (ii) dealers' ideas have to change before 'the worker goes to his factory by car'?
f. What is meant by a 'standardised repair charge'? How would this affect the car-owner?
g. Why was Morris concerned about 'after-sales service'?

# 7 Coal, 1920–38

In 1914 the coal industry could look back on a century of expansion.

Increased demand from abroad was largely responsible for this expansion. In 1913 exports were 98 million tons; in value they were over 10% of total exports of British produce.

The expanding demand could be met only by working less fertile seams, and the increasing exhaustion of the accessible coal was raising the cost of production. A time must come when output can be maintained only if demand is unaffected by rising prices, or if those in the industry accept lower wages and profits.

In 1924–6 consumption was lower than in 1913. The main causes of this stagnation were the economies in the use of coal and the introduction of alternative sources of power. Improvements in boiler and furnace technique led to the extraction of maximum energy from the fuel burnt. The generation of electricity by water power led to a displacement of coal.

There was a revolution in road transport; this retarded railway development. By 1932 40% of the world's mercantile tonnage was dependent on oil. The navies became almost wholly oil-burning.

In 1938 home consumption was slightly less than in 1913 in spite of the rise in population and in industrial production as a whole. This can be attributed mainly to economies in coal consumption and to the use of substitute fuels. The consumption of household coal rose very little, because of the more economical grates, and the use of gas and electricity for heating.

G. C. Allen, *British Industries and their organisation*, 1960.

# Comment

Britain's economic success in modern industry had been built on King Coal and King Cotton (Book I, Section 2). Coal had been the only fuel, and factories using steam power had to be built near, or on, coalfields. Hence the position of the industrial centres. (See Document 19.)

Coal was not used only in British factories. It was used to move British and foreign shipping. It was exported to many countries, particularly to Canada, South America, Scandinavia and the developing countries of the Empire. British ships brought back wheat or some other import. The cost of the voyage out was paid for by the coal exporter, which meant that imports were cheaper.

After 1920 the industry declined. New fuels, such as oil, electricity and gas, reduced the world demand for coal; the newer and more mechanised pits of the U.S.A., Poland and Germany produced coal more cheaply than did the older British pits. The higher prices following the return to the Gold Standard (Document 4) made matters worse. Britain's coal industry had a decreasing share of a dwindling world market.

# Questions

a. Why was the coal industry so important in 1914: (i) as an export industry; (ii) as a domestic fuel?
b. Why did its success lead to increasing costs of production?
c. How could increased costs be affected by: (i) prices; (ii) wages?
d. Why would it prove difficult to: (i) raise prices; (ii) lower wages? (See Document 31.)
e. Give five reasons for a reduction in the demand for coal in 1926.
f. How did (i) the motor-car, (ii) oil-burning ships affect the demand for coal?
g. Give three reasons why the average householder bought less coal in 1938.
h. What effect did the return to the Gold Standard have on the price of and demand for British coal? (See Document 4.)

# 8 Cotton — The Free Trade Case in the New Century

For the very perfection of the textile and other machinery by which England won her industrial leadership has enabled it to be worked fairly well by backward races. Little more than mere order and organised discipline will go a long way towards success, where the same tasks are performed by modern machinery, 'which does most of the thinking itself'. Thus England is at a steadily increasing relative disadvantage in trading, not merely with people like the Japanese, who can assimilate every part of work of an advanced factory, but also with places where there are abundant supplies of low-grade labour, organised by a relatively small number of able and skilled men of a higher race.

Consequently England will not be able to hold her own against other nations by the mere sedulous practice of familiar processes. These are being reduced to such mechanical routine by her own, and still more by American, ingenuity that an Englishman's labour in them will not continue long to count for very much more than that of an equally energetic man of a more backward race. Of course, the Englishman has access to relatively larger and cheaper stores of capital than anyone else. But England's place among the nations in the future must depend on the extent to which she retains industrial leadership. She cannot be *the* leader, but she may be a leader.

Many of the sons of manufacturers (are) content to follow mechanically the lead given by their fathers. They work shorter hours and exert themselves less to obtain new practical ideas than their fathers had done; thus a part of England's leadership was destroyed rapidly.

Alfred Marshall, *Official Papers by Alfred Marshall*, ed. Keynes, 1926.

# Comment

Cotton was one of the main industries in Britain in the 19th century. In this industry many small firms in competition with each other employed over a million workers. The leaders of the industry were believers in Free Trade (Book I, Document 38).

The author of this extract was Alfred Marshall, a famous economist. The Government asked him to advise the Treasury during the Tariff Reform Campaign (1903–5). He came out strongly on the side of Free Trade, even though, as he saw, this was sometimes harmful to certain British industries.

British technical skills had built machinery (Book I, Document 5), and British capital loaned abroad (Document 37) meant that other countries could obtain these machines. For reasons explained in the extract the textile and other industries would suffer from this new competition.

Marshall asked that British industrialists, scientists, capitalists and workpeople should recognise that some of our older industries were going to suffer. He asked that they should develop some of the newer industries, as Germany and the U.S.A. were doing. It is unfortunate that Britain did not do so as rapidly as did the other countries.

# Questions

a. Why could 'backward races' work the textile machinery?
b. Why were these countries at an advantage in labour costs?
c. How would such development affect the demand for British textiles?
d. What advantage did England have over the backward races?
e. How had the 'sons of manufacturers' behaved in regard to: (i) the hours worked; (ii) their development of new ideas?
f. What evidence is there that Britain had lost her position of the world's industrial leader?
g. Using Documents 5 and 6, show how British capital might have been employed to maintain Britain's 'leadership'. Who, according to Marshall, was to blame for this?
h. How did the return to the Gold Standard (Document 4) affect the demand for British textiles?

3a. This was drawn by an American who entitled it 'The invasion of England by American cyclists'.

3b. Oxford Circus, about 1910. The traffic problem is not new.

# Comment

The bicycle began as a 'bone shaker' with different-size wheels. The introduction of the rubber tyre and of two wheels of the same size made cycling easier and more popular. The industry grew (Document 10) as the demand for bicycles grew. Plate 3a gives an idea of how easy and pleasant it was to go by bicycle. People travelled to work, rode out into the countryside, shopped or visited friends more easily with the aid of a bicycle.

The development of the petrol engine (Documents 6 and 11) was very rapid. Plate 3b shows some aspects of this development. There are buses, lorries, taxi-cabs and private cars. People, materials and goods were carried more quickly, farther and more cheaply than previously. It also meant, as the plate shows, overcrowded roads (see also Document 11).

# Questions

a. Why could people live farther away from their place of work if they had a bicycle or a car? How did this lead to the development of suburbs? (See Document 11.)

b. How do these plates illustrate increased opportunities for use of leisure time?

c. Why would many new roads be required because of the development of the petrol engine?

d. How would the shoppers have gone to town before the petrol engine was invented? (See Book I, Document 12.) How does Plate 3b help to explain the decline in the railway industry?

e. If the people hadn't gone to the large town shopping centre, where might they have bought their goods? Why did the development of the petrol engine lead to the growth of shopping centres? (See also Document 24.)

# 9 The Steam-turbine Engine

The object of the Company is to provide the necessary capital for testing the application of Mr. Parsons's well-known steam turbine to the propulsion of vessels.

It is anticipated that with turbines of, say, 1,000 horse-power and upwards, the consumption of steam will be less than with the best condensing engines.

The cost of a steam turbine will be less than that of an ordinary marine engine. The space occupied by the turbines will be very much less than that occupied by ordinary engines, thus largely increasing the carrying capacity of the vessel. The reduction in the amount of vibration admits of a diminution in the weight of the hull, which under the present system must be stronger and heavier than will be necessary under the new system.

Another important feature is the reduced size and weight of the shaft and propeller. This will facilitate duplication and repair, and enable spare parts to be carried on an extent not hitherto practicable, but will also admit of screw-propelled vessels being used for navigating shallow waters, where at present only paddle steamers can be employed.

The merits of the proposed system may be summarized thus: increased speed, increased carrying power of vessel, increased economy in steam consumption, reduced initial cost, reduced weight of machinery, reduced cost of attendance on machinery, diminished cost of upkeep of machinery, largely reduced vibration, and reducing size and weight of screw propeller and shafting.

It is to provide funds for the complete and exhaustive testing of the new system that the Company has been formed.

A. Richardson, *The evolution of the Parsons Steam Turbine*, 1911.

# Comment

In the 19th century there were a number of changes in sea transport from the 'clipper', with its large sails, to the steam engine, first used in iron boats. By the 1880s steel had replaced iron.

Britain depended on overseas trade and it was natural that she should have a large merchant navy. British shipbuilding yards used British iron and steel and the British steam engine to establish an early supremacy in shipbuilding. Foreign ship-owners bought English ships.

It is not surprising, then, that there would be inventions in shipbuilding. It was hoped that the steam turbine would replace the older steam engine. The advantages of the new engine are clearly stated. In fact this turbine revolutionised the speed of travel and was used in both warships and passenger ships. It was of little use, however, for merchant ships since the engine would not run efficiently at less than 20 knots, and merchant ships were not built for such speeds.

This extract is from the prospectus issued by a company formed by Charles Parsons.

# Questions

a. What invention was to be tested? How do we know that this invention was already being used in industry?
b. How would the turbine affect the consumption of coal?
c. How did the cost of the turbine compare with that of the ordinary engine?
d. How big was the turbine? Why would ship-owners welcome this?
e. Why would the turbine require a lighter vessel? Why would this please the ship-owner?
f. How did the turbine affect the size of the shaft and propeller? Give four reasons why this would be welcome to ship-owners.
g. The advantages of the engine appear to be obvious. Why, then, was a company to be formed?
h. Darby (Book I, Document 7), and other early industrialists, had obtained money without forming companies. Why was this not possible for Parsons and other later industrialists?

# 10 The Bicycle Industry

Two immediate results of the boom of 1895 were the importation of foreign cycles — especially American — and the expansion of the home industry [Plate 3a]:

1. The American cycles proved unreliable and have never since obtained any considerable market in England.

2. A vast quantity of automatic machinery was introduced to produce a reliable bicycle at a low price.

3. The London firms were unable to withstand the high equipped Midland firms.

The 'Cycle Manufacturers' do not make their own supplies of tyres, wheel rims, chains, accessories — bells, lamps, etc.

(i) The 'parts' and 'accessories' are purchased from firms who specialise, e.g. Dunlop Tyre Company for tyres, rims, pumps, etc.; Lucas Ltd. for lamps, bells etc.; Perry and Company for cycle chains.

Traders testify to the increasing specialisation of the industry. Considerable plant is necessary and the large investment of fixed capital would not be profitable unless the producing firm can ensure a large and fairly constant output. The quantities required by individual 'cycle manufacturers' would not justify the outlay of capital for independent plants. It is more profitable to purchase supplies of these parts from firms specialising in certain kinds of them. The centre for the manufacture of accessories and parts is Birmingham.

(ii) The 'Cycle Manufacturers' purchase their supplies of steel tubes, bars, wire, accessories, etc. and thence produce the finished cycle. This branch of the industry is centred at Coventry. All the leading cycle-makers produce motor cycles as well as cycles and carriers. The present tendency is to include the manufacture of automobiles also. . . .

G. B. Carter, 'The cycle industry', *Seasonal Trades*, 1912.

# Comment

The bicycle had been invented in the 1860s but it did not become popular until a number of inventions had been made. Perhaps the most important was the invention of the pneumatic tyre by Dunlop of Belfast. From the beginning there was a good deal of foreign competition, the result of foreign development (Section 1), and the transport revolution (Document 9).

As has already been seen (Book I, Document 24), the living standards of the people were rising throughout the 19th century. The falling prices of food (after 1870), and stable wage rates, meant that many people continued to enjoy a high standard even during the 'Great Depression'. One of the indications of this increased standard of living was the purchase of bicycles.

# Questions

a. How had the boom of 1895 affected: (i) the import of foreign cycles; (ii) the home industry?

b. How had automatic machinery affected the price of the bicycles? How does this experience compare with that of Morris (Document 6)?

c. Why was this industry an 'assembly' industry? Give the name of three firms who supplied the industry.

d. Why could Dunlop and other firms produce items more efficiently than the bicycle firms? (See also Document 6, Question c.)

e. Why did these firms establish factories around Birmingham?

f. How does the document help to explain: (i) the location of the car industry; (ii) the continued growth of the population of the Midlands?

g. The industry grew. What does this tell us of the standard of living enjoyed in this country?

h. How did the bicycle affect: (i) the movement of population away from the older parts of the towns (Plate 4); (ii) the use of leisure time (Plate 3a)?

# 11 The Motor-car

By 1923 British manufacturers were using mass-production methods [Plate 2a], and the car was becoming reasonably trustworthy: one seldom saw a car drawn up at the side of the road with the driver underneath as he tinkered away. In 1923 cord fabric was first used for tyres, prolonging their lives by five thousand miles. By 1924 the increasing use of cars by week-enders brought the Baby Car into the market. The 'Austin Seven' cost £165. Then came the solid-tyred Trojan four-seater at £125, and the Morris Minor.

It was not only the lower price of the mass-produced car that recommended it, but the readiness with which spare parts could be supplied.

Buses began to run on new routes: as cities spread out, so the local buses extended their itineraries. The long-distance charabanc challenged the railway for speed and comfort, and made night journeys from the north and west of England to London. The charabanc opened up rural districts which were still almost inaccessible by rail.

The cheap car and the new bus service brought ribbon-building. This meant stringing houses along main roads instead of building them in compact village-like masses. For the tenants, the advantage was obvious: access to the road and an uninterrupted country view from their back windows.

Saturday and Sunday evenings — when cars from London and other big cities were hurrying home in an unbroken stream, trying to overtake one another on tricky, tortuous roads — and the work-day rush-hour in Town in foggy weather were the bloodiest times.

Robert Graves and Alan Hodge, *The Long Weekend*, 1950.

# Comment

This document shows the advantages of mass production — a cheap car easily supplied with spare parts. The Ford and Morris factories depended on a large sale, and they got this by lowering the price of their product; a larger number of people could afford to buy. Week-enders enjoyed the countryside and seaside, visited their families and friends and thought that 'hurrying home in an unbroken stream' on tricky tortuous roads was worth while.

Road transport, especially lorries and buses, had a number of effects. People could now live away from their place of work, instead of crowding around the factories; and factories need not be built near railway lines or ports, since lorries could carry the raw material and finished product.

The railways were built with 'ways' for the engines. The motor-car manufacturers only provided the 'engine' of transport and not 'the way'. Whereas private enterprise had built both the railway engines and the track, the Government, at national and local level, built new roads, and maintained the old ones.

# Questions

a. Why were car prices falling 'by 1923'? (See also Documents 6 and 10.)
b. Why do 'trustworthy' and 'prolonging' help to explain the increase in the number of car-owners?
c. William Morris (Document 6) had spoken about 'spare parts'. How had their availability affected car ownership?
d. How did the development of bus services affect the growth of suburbs? Who had been able to live there before? Why?
e. Why did 'the tenants' welcome 'ribbon-building'?
f. Why were roads crowded on Saturday and Sunday evenings?
g. What effect had the ownership of a car on family life?
h. Why did the division between town and country break down in this period?

# 12 The Early Fliers

Two R.A.F. fliers, Captain Alcock and Lieutenant Brown, made the first successful flight between America and northern Europe. When Charles Lindbergh made his flight in 1927, it was assumed even in Britain that this was the first time the Atlantic had been flown.

The general opinion about Atlantic flights was that they had more scientific than commercial value. No freight could be carried in such small aircraft and the strain of such long distances was bound to exhaust the pilots. A great deal of improvement was needed before Atlantic flights could become commercially practicable.

Ordinary commercial flying developed rapidly. In 1922 aeroplanes began to be used for sky-advertising; plans were made for using luminous smoke by night and coloured smoke by day. Aeroplanes were also employed to fly low with advertisement streamers — usually for such commodities as Bile Beans.

In 1922 flying had not yet become popular among business men who travelled to and from the Continent. They complained that machines were not comfortable; and when more luxurious 'air-expresses' were introduced, they complained of the time lost on motor connections between the airports and the cities. The speed of aeroplanes — then only one hundred miles an hour — did not allow much time to be saved over so short a distance. Passenger air-traffic was seasonal; summer vacations, when American tourists used the air, were the most profitable time.

By 1923 many improvements had been introduced. The new steel aircraft inspired far more confidence than the early wood-and-wire contraptions. Air-expresses were flying in all kinds of weather; experiments were made in night flying — until then direction-finding equipment had only served for day flying. In 1924 a unified system of radio communication was put into force throughout Europe, to assist in direction finding.

Robert Graves and Alan Hodge, *The Long Weekend*, 1950.

# Comment

The aeroplane was invented at the end of the 19th century, and Rolls and Lanchester were pioneers in this as in the motor-car industry. However, even as late as 1924, the aeroplane was not a popular or common method of transport, as the document shows.

Many people tried to popularise it. The newspapers offered large prizes for competitions. Alcock and Brown won such a competition.

As the document shows, the usefulness of early air travel was very limited, whether for carrying freight or passengers. The development of the aeroplane was possible because of the technical and scientific discoveries which had already taken place, e.g. in engineering and in the motor-car industry. The aeroplanes led to further developments in engineering, radio and airframe industries.

# Questions

*a.* Who made the first flight across the Atlantic?
*b.* Why were business men not very interested in such flights?
*c.* How did the advertising industry use the aeroplane?
*d.* How fast did aeroplanes go in 1922? Why did business men not use them 'to and from the continent'?
*e.* How did the aeroplane affect tourists?
*f.* Give two ways in which flying became safer in 1923–4.
*g.* How did the development of air transport affect: (i) the radio industry; (ii) international co-operation?
*h.* Sir Joseph Swan had spoken of the need for higher education in 1903 (Document 3). How did the development of the transport industry (Documents 9–12) increase this need? (Think of design, research, technicians, workpeople, management.)

4a. Crosby Row, London, before the first world war.

4b. A workers' housing estate in Yorkshire, laid out on a circular plan.

# Comment

The housing conditions shown in Plate 4a are typical of those described in Document 13. Many families with low incomes (Documents 22 and 26) had little money to spend on rent. People with money to invest could expect a high interest from industrial investment at home (Documents 5 and 6) and from investment overseas (Document 37); if they invested their money in housing they could obtain a good interest from the high rents which the upper classes could pay (Documents 21 and 23); the low rents which many poor families could afford would not provide a sufficiently high return to attract capital to building adequate houses for the poorer classes.

A high death-rate and a good deal of sickness were the immediate effects of these conditions; the housewife was soon discouraged from trying to keep her home clean; her children grew up in conditions which did not help their educational development (see Plate 12a).

Plate 4b illustrates the conditions described in Document 14. Here there has been an attempt to plan a housing estate: there are fields near by; houses have gardens. In these houses lived the type of child pictured in Plate 12c.

# Questions

a. Why was there more danger of disease spreading in the London houses (Plate 4a) than in the Yorkshire houses (Plate 4b)?

b. More people lived in a square mile of slum territory than lived on a square mile of new housing. Why? Why did this result in the outward spread of towns?

c. Why did the people living in the Yorkshire estate need some method of transport more than did the people living in the London slum: (i) for getting to work; (ii) for doing their shopping? (See also Plates 3a and 3b.)

d. Which house would be worth a higher rent — the London slum or the Yorkshire house? If people could not afford to pay high rents in London, how could they afford to live in the better housing of the estate?

e. How does Plate 4b help you to understand the decrease in infant mortality (Document 15)?

# 13 Housing Conditions for the Poor, 1883

First, the information given does not refer to selected cases. Secondly, there has been absolutely no exaggeration. This must be to every Christian heart a loud and bitter cry, appealing for the help which it is the supreme mission of the Church to supply.

You have to penetrate courts reeking with poisonous and malodorous gases arising from the accumulations of sewage and refuse scattered in all directions; courts, many of them which the sun never penetrates, which are never visited by a breath of fresh air. You have to ascend rotten staircases. You have to grope your way along dark and filthy passages swarming with vermin. Then you may gain admittance to the dens in which these thousands of beings, who belong as much as you to the race for whom Christ died, herd together. Eight feet square — that is about the average size of very many of these rooms. Walls and ceilings are black with the accretions of filth which have gathered upon them in the boards overhead; it is running down the walls; it is everywhere. A window is half stuffed with rags or covered by boards to keep out wind and rain; you look out upon the roofs and ledges of lower tenements, and discover that the sickly air which finds its way into the room has to pass over the putrefying carcases of dead cats or birds. As to furniture — you may perchance discover a broken chair, the tottering relics of an old bedstead or the mere fragment of a table; but more commonly you will find rude substitutes for these things in the shape of rough boards resting upon bricks, an old hamper or box turned upside down, or more frequently still, nothing but rubbish and rags. [See Plate 4a.]

Rev. Andrew Mearns, *The bitter cry of outcast London*, 1883.

4c. Children sleeping in slum conditions.

## Comment

This document is an extract from a pamphlet published by a Congregationalist minister in 1883. It was a sign of an awakening of public interest in sanitary conditions, where Chadwick had, very largely, failed (Book I, Section 4). Some thirty years later, in spite of acts sponsored by Disraeli, and the reform of local government, conditions were as bad as when Chadwick was writing.

## Questions

*a.* Why could the author of this extract claim that his description was one which could be applied to many areas?

*b.* Who, according to the author, should be appalled?

*c.* Why was there a danger of disease as a result of conditions outside the houses?

*d.* What was the average size of a room? Compare this with the size of a room in your own home.

*e.* Why was there a danger of disease as a result of conditions inside the home?

*f.* Why were people forced to live in these conditions?

*g.* These slums would have to be cleared and new houses built. Why would this require: (i) legislation; (ii) a more active local authority; (iii) increased taxation?

# 14 Council Housing in the 1930s

The first section where 938 families will ultimately live in municipal flats, was declared open by Alderman J. Badley.

At the opening . . . the Chairman of the Housing Committee (Alderman H. A. Blackah) described the Quarry Hill development.

He spoke of children's playgrounds and gardens and many other amenities that will be available when the scheme is complete. There will be five children's playgrounds on the estate. More than half the area — is set aside for open spaces and playgrounds.

'We believe that the Lord Mayor will yet see roses growing at Quarry Hill,' he said. This observation drew a smile from Alderman Badley, for he knew Quarry Hill when it was one of the worst slums in Leeds.

Alderman Blackah said that anybody with knowledge of the housing problem would not dispute that such tenement developments as at Quarry Hill must take place.

Every flat has a living room facing the sun, and a back-to-back range that will give warmth to the living room and scullery. Until the communal laundry is working, rent rebate will be charged to tenants. A charge for the use of the laundry will be included in the rent.

Alderman Blackah said that these were the finest tenements built for the wage earners in this country.

The Rev. Charles Jenkinson, Chairman of the Housing Committee when the Quarry Hill Flats scheme was launched, said in his speech that in 1932 he and Councillor F. Barraclough visited Vienna, where they saw the flats run by the municipality.

'The origin of the Quarry Hill flats took place on that morning in the summer of 1932,' he said.

*Yorkshire Evening Post*, 30th March 1938.

# Comment

The document describes the opening of a new housing estate in 1938 built by Leeds Corporation on a cleared slum area, Quarry Hill.

A large minority of people (see Document 22) who were underemployed, unemployed or poorly paid could not afford an economic rent. So they could never get a house, but were forced to share one with other families. Hence the overcrowding (Document 13). It was for such people that council housing was proposed. Houses would be built by the local council and rents fixed at a low level, and the local council would recover its losses out of the rates, i.e. the better-off would help the poor. (See Document 35.)

# Questions

*a.* Who had built the 'flats'? How does this show that state activity was increasing?
*b.* Why would children welcome the development at Quarry Hill?
*c.* Why did Alderman Badley smile? Why could he hope that there would be a decrease in the death-rate at Quarry Hill?
*d.* Why would the older tenants welcome the development?
*e.* Where had the councillor seen municipal flats in 1932?
*f.* Compare the conditions in these houses with those described in Document 13.
*g.* Why could the municipal authority build such flats (for wage-earners) while private landlords could not?
*h.* Good housing for the lower class required regulation and subsidies. Find out: (i) when the first Town and Country Planning Act was passed; (ii) how the Chamberlain Housing Act affected council-house rents.

# 15 Neville Chamberlain and Public Health

The Ministry was responsible not only for housing, but for civil pensions and National Health Insurance, for the administration of the Poor Law and the Public Health Services. Much of the legislation has an important place in the development of the Welfare State.

The National Health Insurance Act of 1928, greatly extended health insurance benefits; giving new benefits of specialist advice and surgical treatment to members of Approved Societies, softening the requirements to help the unemployed, married women and the old, and, in all, bringing added help to some sixteen and a half million men and women workers. In four years 440 more Infant Welfare Centres were opened and 300 more ante-natal clinics, while the number of practising midwives increased by 860. The infant mortality rate, 132 per 1000 live births in 1906, 75 in 1924, was 65 in 1928. The maternal mortality rate stayed high and Chamberlain, mainly through the Midwives and Maternity Homes Act, 1926, by supervising Nursing Homes through Local Authorities by the Act of 1927, and by greatly increased expenditure on the Maternity and Child Welfare Services, worked tirelessly to reduce it.

There was legislation on clean food, clean water and clean air as well as the important Public Health Act of 1925. The 'policy of sewage' inspired by Disraeli was in good hands.

Chamberlain too was an insatiable traveller as all Ministers of Health have to be. And perhaps only another Minister of Health can really appreciate with him the exciting study of new methods in hospitals and clinics and the pleasure of meeting the men and women at work there. Chamberlain, as he went round, was concerned to test the adequacy of local administration. Larger authorities with greater executive and supervisory powers were needed, and Chamberlain argued tenaciously for the measure that became the Local Government Act, 1929.

Iain Macleod, *Neville Chamberlain*, 1961.

# Comment

This is from Iain Macleod's biography of Neville Chamberlain. Mr. Macleod (a former Minister of Health) had a special appreciation of Chamberlain's work as Minister of Health.

The extract shows clearly the growth of government activity in the field of Public Health.

Infant mortality is often called 'the indicator of the nation's health'. If a high proportion of children die before their first birthday the nation is clearly less healthy than when only a small proportion die. The improvement in the nation's health is shown in the document.

This improvement was due, in part, to government action, so there was a demand for more government measures.

# Questions

*a.* What was the Ministry of Health 'responsible for'?

*b.* '. . . in the development of the Welfare State'. How did the National Health Insurance Act, 1928, improve on previous Acts?

*c.* How did the work of Neville Chamberlain help expectant mothers?

*d.* How did Chamberlain try to reduce the maternal mortality rate?

*e.* Why was 'local administration' so important? What services mentioned in this document would these authorities supervise? (See also Document 35.)

*f.* Infant mortality is the key to the nation's health. Give two reasons from the document for the decline in infant mortality. Can you suggest two more? (See Documents 14 and 24.)

*g.* Why did Chamberlain's activity (Questions (*b*)–(*d*)) lead to increased taxation?

*h.* Why does the document mention Disraeli? What Acts passed between 1874 and 1880 were improved by Chamberlain?

# 16 Family Allowances

Eleanor's sense of justice was disturbed: men and women appeared to be doing equal work, the women received less pay . . . men have families to keep. (This barrier) to the achievement of 'equal pay for equal work' could only be removed by the acceptance of family allowances.

The First World War provided the case for family allowances. Family disruption was a sad business, but here was a new security in the lives of working mothers; a family income in relation to the burden of family expense. The separation allowances were meagre. A weekly allowance of 12s. 6d. for the mother, 5s. for the first child and 3s. 6d. for each subsequent child represented spending power in the mother's own hands; hers by right.

But what struck her as the war years rolled by was the physical well-being and maternal efficiency which could be yielded by small sums of money entrusted to the mother. *Of course* family allowances were the answer to the 'equal pay' impasse. She had long suspected it. *Now she knew.*

The opposition came from widely diffused sources. Economists and Liberals of the laissez-faire school used counter-arguments reminiscent of those which Malthus had brought to bear against the outdoor relief allowances of the unreformed Poor Law. This argument appealed to the Conservative Party, where dislike of any redistribution of income was a natural response to a proposal to socialise family dependency. Many members of the Labour Party visualised a measure which might complicate the traditional conception of a standard wage.

. . . if ever one person was responsible for a major reform, Eleanor was responsible for family allowances. Plimsoll did not achieve his Plimsoll line in complete isolation: nor did Belisha erect his beacons single-handed; Lansbury could scarcely have constructed his Lido without public support. Nevertheless if there had been no Eleanor it is difficult not to conclude that there would have been no Family Allowance Act in 1945. It was *her* victory.

Mary Stocks, *Eleanor Rathbone*, 1949.

4d. One of the first London mothers to draw the family allowance in 1946.

## Comment

This extract is from the biography of Eleanor Rathbone by Mrs. Mary Stocks. Eleanor Rathbone was a Feminist (see Document 20), anxious that women should be treated as equals with and by men. Women did not (nor, in many cases, do they today) receive equal pay for equal work (paragraph 1). Eleanor Rathbone argued that a system of family allowances would overcome this difficulty — the married men's pay would be supplemented by a family allowance.

## Questions

*a.* Why did men receive higher pay than women doing equal work?

*b.* How could this 'barrier' be removed?

*c.* When did the Government first pay family allowances? To whom were they given?

*d.* What was the total allowance made to a mother with: (i) four children; (ii) six children?

*e.* What was the result of such allowances? Compare the life of a soldier's family of four children with the life of a family in Document 22.

*f.* Why did (i) Liberals and Economists, (ii) the Conservative Party, oppose the principle of family allowances in peace-time?

*g.* Why were trade unionists against family allowances?

*h.* What does the document mean by 'a redistribution of income'? Who would gain and who would lose by this redistribution?

THE MAIN CHANCE.

5a.

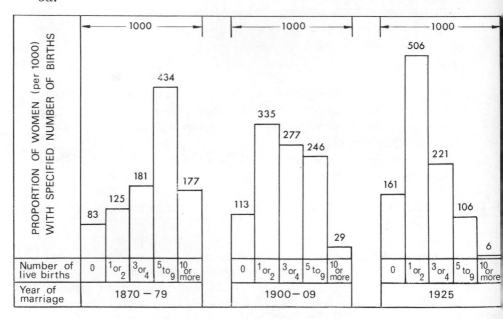

5b.

# Comment

The growth of population in the late 18th and 19th centuries was due largely to the decline in the death-rate. Many children had been born in early 18th-century families; many of these had died. In the later period more of these children lived (Document 15); the large family was one feature of Victorian life. One such family is shown in Plate 5a.

However, as Plate 5b shows, there was a fall in the birth-rate after 1870. Along with this fall there was a rise in the expectation of life; women had, on average, died at 45 in 1850; by 1930 they were living, on average, for over 65 years. This meant that women spent fewer years rearing their smaller families than had their parents, and they also had a longer life. This was one of the reasons for the demand for increased opportunities for women to go to work (see Documents 20 and 24).

# Questions

a. Draw histograms using red for 1870–9, blue for 1900–9 and black for 1925.
b. Of women married in 1870–9, 611 had more than 5 children. What was the number of children for 612 women married in 1900–9 and for 667 women married in 1925?
c. How do these figures help you to understand that mothers found life easier at the end of the period? (See also Document 24.)
d. The children in Plates 12a–c were born at different times in this period. How do the figures in Plate 5b help you to understand the improvement in the appearance of the children?
e. Why would the emigration of one child lead to a lonelier life for mothers first married in 1925 than for the mothers first married 1870–9?

# 17 Sweated Industries, 1906

The following letter is printed because it represents the experience of a host of similar sufferers. For every statement made she is prepared to produce chapter and verse.

April 17th, 1906.

Sir,

The following is an account of my past experience as a City machinist. I sought work from firms now in existence and obtained work at these prices:

| | | |
|---|---|---|
| Flannel and cotton chemises, plain bands with trimming on them and on sleeves . . . . . | 1s. | doz. |
| Flannel and cotton small children's chemises and knickers, no trimming . . . . . . | 8d. | ,, |
| Flannel and cotton nightdresses, with insertion and frills on neck and sleeves . . . . . | 2s. 9d. | ,, |
| Flannelette bathing gowns, trimmed with braid . . | 3s. | ,, |
| Ladies' flannel and cotton shirts, plain . . . | 1s. 9d. | ,, |
| The velvet ones . . . . . . . | 2s. 3d. | ,, |
| and | | |
| Ladies' white muslin shirts, trimming down fronts, 1 row each side, tucks in between, making about 20 tucks | 3s. | ,, |

After paying for cotton and railway journey, I had 7s. per week on an average, sometimes less, and paid 5s. for rent; I worked from six a.m. in morning till ten at night, only taking about one hour for my meals. While at warehouses I saw some had notices up that work kept longer than four days would not be paid full price. Work must be counted before taken away, or any deficiency must be paid for. A difficult matter to measure trimmings and count parts in a hurry, especially when you sometimes only had the floor to pack up on.

*Sweated industries*, being a handbook of the *Daily News* exhibition, compiled by Richard M. Smith, 1906.

# Comment

While factory conditions had been improved by legislation and trade union activity, there were, at the beginning of the 20th century, many people working in what were known as the 'sweated industries'. A select committee of the House of Lords reported on these industries (1890), and listed the sweated trades. Matchboxes, clothes, nails and cutlery were cheap goods, easily made, often at home, by married women. These women were willing to work because of low family incomes, but at home they were outside the scope of the factory inspectorate. It was impossible for workers in these trades to be effectively organised in a trade union, and little could be done to improve their conditions.

This letter was written to the Anti-Sweating League formed in 1905. It organised an exhibition of goods produced in the sweated trades and industries in Queen's Hall, London, in 1906. The *Daily News* (later the *News Chronicle*) took up the campaign.

# Questions

*a.* How much was the worker paid: (i) for each chemise; (ii) for each nightdress?

*b.* Why did the worker have to pay for 'railway journey'? (Who gave her the work? Where did she do it?)

*c.* How many hours per day did she work? Compare this with Factory Regulations in 1833 (Book I, Document 19).

*d.* How did firms punish slow workers? Why did this affect: (i) the sick; (ii) the older workers?

*e.* Why might the worker and the employer disagree on 'trimmings'?

*f.* Why could these items be made in the home?

*g.* Why did some people welcome work like this and accept the conditions? (See Documents 13 and 22.)

*h.* How did the Liberals attack this problem in the Trades Board Acts between 1909 and 1913?

# 18 Labour Exchanges, 1909

There are two general defects in the industrial position of this country, the lack of mobility of labour and the lack of information about all these questions of unemployment. For both defects the labour exchanges afford a remedy. Modern industry is national. Transport and communication knit the country together as no country has ever been knitted before. Labour alone has not profited by this improved organisation. The method by which labour obtains its market today is the old method, hawking labour about from place to place, and treating a job as a thing which places a man under an obligation when he has got it. The movement of labour when it is necessary should be effected with the least friction, the least suffering, the least loss of time and of status to the individual who is called upon by the force of economic conditions to move. The result of the policy will be to make it easy for him to move the moment the ordinary economic events arise which make movement necessary. Labour exchanges will not to any large extent create new employment. What they are going to do is to organise the existing labour by which we cannot help raising the general standard of economic life.

Labour exchanges are indispensable to any system of unemployment insurance, since it is not possible to make the distinction between the vagrant and the loafer on the one hand and the bona fide workman on the other, except in some elaborate and effective system of testing willingness to work such as is afforded by the system of labour exchanges. I shall tomorrow have an opportunity of asking the permission of the House to introduce this Bill, and we present it to the House as a piece of social machinery, nothing more and nothing less, the need of which has long been apparent, and the want of which has been widely and cruelly felt by large numbers of our fellow countrymen.

Winston Churchill in the House of Commons, 19th May 1909.

# Comment

This is an extract from a speech made by Winston Churchill on 19th May 1909. He was addressing the House of Commons on the subject of Labour Exchanges. Earlier in the speech he had shown that the idea of such Exchanges was supported by both Majority and Minority Reports of the Poor Law Commission, trade-union leaders, the Labour Party, economists from both Free Trade and Tariff Reform camps and leaders of the Conservative Party. As Mr. Churchill showed in his speech, Britain was now going to imitate Germany, Austria, Switzerland, France, Belgium and Norway, who had had such Exchanges for some years.

# Questions

*a.* What two things made 'modern industry national'?
*b.* How did a man find a new job before 1909? Why did this lead to a loss of status and of time?
*c.* Take the examples of unemployment in Jarrow and of growing industry in Oxford (see Documents 6 and 7). How would a system of Labour Exchanges 'make it easier for him to move' from one place to another?
*d.* What, according to Mr. Churchill, would Labour Exchanges not do? Can you say why such Exchanges led to some new employment? (See also Document 36.)
*e.* Why were Labour Exchanges ' "indispensable" to any system of unemployment insurance'?
*f.* What would make it necessary for a man to move?
*g.* Name three Acts by which the Liberals (1904–14) helped the unemployed.
*h.* Why did this Act lead to increased taxation?

# 19 Coal-mining in the 1930s

Our civilisation is founded on coal. The machines that keep us alive, and the machines that make the machines are all dependent upon coal. In the Western World the coal-miner is second in importance only to the man who ploughs the soil.

When you go down a coal-mine it is important to try and get to the coal face when the 'fillers' are at work. Most of the things one imagines in hell are there — heat, noise, confusion, darkness, foul air, and above all, unbearably cramped space. You see opposite you a shiny black wall three or four feet high. This is the coal face. Overhead is the smooth ceiling made by the rock from which the coal has been cut; underneath is the rock again, so that the gallery you are in is only as high as the ledge of coal itself, probably not much more than a yard. You cannot see very far, because the fog of coal dust throws back the beam of your lamp, but you can see on either side of you the line of half-naked kneeling men, one to every four or five yards, driving their shovels under the fallen coal and flinging it swiftly over their left shoulders on to the conveyor belt. Down this belt a glittering river of coal races constantly — several tons of coal every minute.

They are on the job for seven and a half hours, theoretically without a break, for there is no time 'off'. Actually they snatch a quarter of an hour or so at some time during the shift to eat the food they have brought with them, usually a hunk of bread and dripping and a bottle of cold tea.

George Orwell, *The Road to Wigan Pier*, 1937.

5c. Coal-miner at work in a wet seam at Canderrig colliery (now closed).

## Comment

This is an extract from George Orwell's *The Road to Wigan Pier*. Orwell describes the work of the miners, whose working conditions had hardly improved during 100 years of factory legislation.

## Questions

*a.* Why does Orwell say that 'our civilisation is founded on coal'?

*b.* Why is this less true today than it was in the 1930s? (See also Document 7 and Plate 2.)

*c.* Why is the man who ploughs the soil more valuable than the coal-miner?

*d.* Why does Orwell say that the mine is 'like hell'?

*e.* How high was the ledge of coal? What was 'overhead' and 'underneath'?

*f.* Why were the 'fillers' kneeling? What were they doing?

*g.* How long was the miners' working day? What did they do for meals?

*h.* Draw a diagram, or make a model, to illustrate this extract.

# 20 More Women Go to Work, 1914–39

The women had been acclaimed as patriots, were now represented as vampires who deprive men of their rightful jobs. By Trade Union pressure they were dismissed from engineering, printing, and transport work, and from factories where they had worked on munitions. No Unemployment Benefit scheme was arranged for them. They were expected to become domestic servants. But any girl who had earned good wages in factories and liked the regular hours, the society of other workers, and the strict but impersonal discipline, was reluctant to put herself under the personal domination of 'some old cat' for long hours, little money and complete subservience.

However, more women assistants continued to be employed in shops and offices than before the war — there being no male Trade Union strong enough to exclude them from these trades — and many, who had experience in munition factories, got jobs in the new electrical and wireless industries. They were paid only about two-thirds of the wages that male employees received. Among the middle classes daughters were expected to take up business careers.

More women were going to universities. Oxford admitted them to full membership in 1919. The Cambridge Senate refused to admit women to university membership, but in 1921 granted degree titles to women.

The Sex Disqualification (Removal) Act of 1919 admitted women to many professions, including the Bar. The 'Votes for Women!' cry now gave place to that of 'Equal Pay for Equal Work!' But the industrial magnates and the Trade Union leaders proved to have harder hearts than the politicians: and the discrimination against women continued throughout the period.

Robert Graves and Alan Hodge, *The Long Weekend*, 1950.

# Comment

Women had been trying to get equality of opportunity for the last thirty years of the 19th century. The First World War (1914–18) gave them an opportunity.

The war had changed the social pattern of life, and nowhere was this more true than in the case of women. The 'servant shortage' is an indication of this change. War had also brought technical changes.

The new industries, the civil service, local government gave opportunities for their employment, but there was still a prejudice against women. Once they were married they must leave teaching, the civil service and local government; married or single, they never received equal pay for equal work.

# Questions

a. Why had women been called 'patriots'? What jobs had they been able to do?
b. What happened to them in 1919? Why?
c. What jobs were they 'expected' to do? (See Document 21.) Did they take these jobs? (See Document 23.)
d. What were four benefits of factory work compared with domestic service?
e. Why was there less need for domestic servants?
f. In which three occupations did women get increased employment?
g. What changes in opportunities for women came in: (i) 1919; (ii) 1921?
h. Note Plate 5. Briefly show how (i) newer jobs, (ii) household inventions, (iii) smaller families, (iv) educational opportunities, all played a part in creating a 'freer' life for women.

6a. A family at tea in the 1860s.

6b. East End kitchen, about 1912. The baby and the girl are crying because there is no food.

6c. A more prosperous family having tea, about 1910.

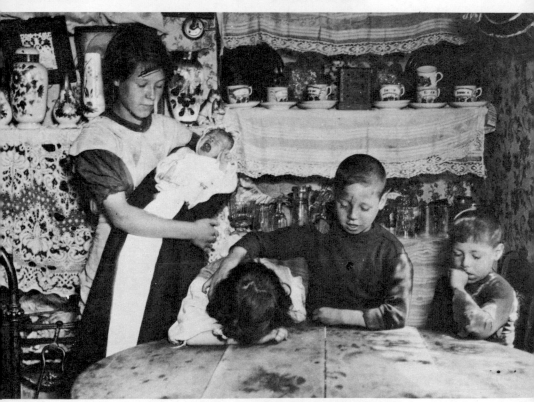

# Comment

These three plates show us part of the homes of two different classes of people. You can see the difference in dress, furniture, and size of the room. Each home has its ornaments and its mantelpiece. (See also Plate 4a again.)

# Questions

*a.* What evidence is there that coal was used for heating in Plate 6a?
*b.* Compare the dress of the families in Plates 6b and 6c.
*c.* Which of the families shown in the plates looks most prosperous? Why?
*d.* How would you expect a modern living-room to differ from those shown in the plates?

# 21 Upper-class Living, 1900

We proceeded to modernise it with a service lift, electric light and a telephone, not as usual a piece of domestic equipment as it now is.

This house when rebuilt contained a large basement, three sitting-rooms, a lounge-hall, and seven bedrooms. All the rooms were warmed by coal fires. There were nursery meals to be carried up and down, hot water to be taken to the bedrooms, and we entertained a good deal in a small way. Yet we found little difficulty in running the house with a staff consisting of a Norland nurse, a parlourmaid, a housemaid and a cook. Later we kept a manservant for £70 a year. The cook earned £28. The Norland nurse's salary was £40. Norland nurses, who were women of the educated classes trained at the Norland Institute, wore a special uniform and were a novelty. Later, while our second child was in the nursery meal stage, we had a between maid.

We spent about 12s. a head each week on food and cleaning materials, which included the cost of come-and-go guests, but not of parties. We bought coal at 15s. a ton, taking six tons at a time, laundry charges were half what they are now, and the cost of the upkeep of a house much less because labour was cheaper, and the rent and upkeep of shops and business premises very much less. There was penny postage, no insurance to pay for domestic servants, stamps on cheques cost 1d. each and, most important of all, Income Tax was but 1s. in the £.

Mrs. C. S. Peel, *Life's Enchanted Cup*, 1933.

# Comment

The increasing wealth (Book I, Document 24) was enjoyed by all. Here is an extract from an autobiography by Mrs. C. S. Peel. She is recalling her childhood, when the family moved into Brompton Square, formerly a squalid area, but becoming fashionable in the late 19th century.

The size of the house, the amount of labour required, the wages paid and the level of taxation, the cost of food, coal and services are all revealing of life at the end of last century.

# Questions

a. In what three ways was the house 'modernised'?
b. How many rooms were in the house? What was 'the basement' used for?
c. What four reasons are given for employing domestic staff?
d. How many staff were employed? What tasks did they perform? How can you tell that the living standard of this family improved? (See 'Later we kept . . .')
e. Why: (i) did they want so much coal; (ii) did this fuel create the demand for some domestic staff? ('All the rooms . . .')
f. Why did (i) wage rates, (ii) food prices (Document 1 and Book I, Document 40) make it easier to keep a house like this?
g. Why was there: (i) no insurance to pay for domestic servants; (ii) such a low level of income tax? (See also Document 15 (g) and Document 16 (h).)
h. Write a short account of a middle-class home today, bringing out the main differences between this home and the one mentioned in the document. (See also Document 24.)

# 22 The Poor, 1900–14

(*a*) A woman told of the struggle when her husband was earning only 17*s*. a week. To make ends meet for a large family was no easy matter. They never had a joint of meat, but occasionally 6*d*. worth of 'meat pieces'. At the birth of a child she employed a woman for a week to nurse her, to whom she gave 5*s*. and her board. As soon as she knew that a child was coming she began saving odd coppers until the 5*s*. was collected. During the time she was nursing her children she lived upon bread and tea. Who can wonder that some of her children died during their first year? [Plate 6b.]

(*b*) How does a working man bring up a family on 20*s*. a week? Assuming that there are four children and that it costs 4*s*. a week to feed a child, there would be but 4*s*. left on which to feed both parents. Four shillings is allowed for food for a child boarded out by Boards of Guardians; it would seem to be a justifiable figure to reckon upon. For a woman with 20*s*. a week it is ridiculously high. If the calculation were made upon half this, the food for the children would amount to 8*s*. To allow the same amount to each parent as to each child would not be an extravagance, and we should arrive at the sum of 12*s*. a week for the food of six people. That would leave 8*s*. for all other expenses. But rent alone may come to 6*s*. or 7*s*., and how could the woman on 20*s*. a week manage with 1*s*., or perhaps 2*s*., for coal, gas, insurance, clothes, cleaning materials and thrift?

(*a*) B. Seebohm Rowntree, *Poverty*, 1901.
(*b*) Mrs. Pember Reeves, *Round about a Pound a week*, 1913.

## Comment

Lloyd George spoke of unemployment in Document 27. These extracts illustrate the problems of the labouring classes. In 1913 the average wage for an unskilled worker was, as the title of the book indicates, *Round about a Pound a week*. This was an improvement on the 17*s*. mentioned in the Rowntree survey (1901).

The extract shows some of the ways in which money was spent — rent, heating, food, etc.

6d. Inside the home of a poor man, about 1912.

The lowly paid worker was unable to afford the contributory insurance scheme introduced by Lloyd George in 1911. Lloyd George claimed (Document 46) that the 'better-off classes' did not realise the 'sufferings of the unemployed'. He himself may be accused of not fully appreciating the poverty of some employed workmen.

# Questions

a. '... earning only 17s. a week'. How did such earnings affect: (i) the rent this family could afford (see Documents 13 and 14); (ii) the meals they had?

b. Why did the mother save 5s.?

c. What did the mother eat while she was feeding the newly born infant?

d. 'Who can wonder ...' How do these extracts help to explain the high infant mortality figures (Document 15)?

e. Why would the family in extract (b) be better off under the Poor Law?

f. How would a system of Family Allowances (Document 16) help families with low incomes?

g. Why did these families not take out cut insurance policies (Document 33)?

h. How would (i) subsidised housing (Document 14), (ii) improved maternity care (Document 15) help these families? Why would this mean a 'redistribution of income' (Document 16)?

# 23 Changes in Money Values, 1920s

London is a striking witness to the changes which have taken place in the life of the educated classes. With few exceptions great houses have become clubs, institutions, offices; their former owners can no longer afford their upkeep. The roomy houses in which Victorian and Edwardian families lived have been divided into upper and lower parts, reconstructed to form flats, or turned into boarding houses, private hotels or hostels. Many girls, who would in pre-War days have married into a nice little house and kept a nice little household, live in a minute flat and afford, perhaps, a nurse, and themselves act as cook and house parlourmaid, with or without the assistance of a 'daily'.

Until 1912, when prices began to rise slightly, it was possible for a competent housewife, even in a servant-keeping house, to provide an early cup of tea, a breakfast dish and the usual toast, butter and marmalade, an 11 o'clock refresher for the maids, a substantial luncheon which was also the nursery and servants' dinner, a simple tea and a three course dinner for eight people, two of whom dined late, for 10s. per head per week;

In a two-to-four servant middle-class household (including a nurse) the standard of living expected by the maids was not as high as it is now.

During the War the cost of food rose by 129 per cent above 1914 prices, and in 1920, the year of the highest prices, to 191 per cent above 1914 prices. At the time that I write these words — March 1933 — it is again possible, given clever management, to provide plain food of the kind to which middle class people are now accustomed at the 10s. rate.

Mrs. C. S. Peel, *Life's Enchanted Cup*, 1933.

# Comment

The First World War (1914–18) saw the end of a period in which the upper classes had enjoyed *Life's Enchanted Cup* — the title of Mrs. Peel's autobiography, from which this extract is taken. Very many of the upper classes lived on fixed incomes — the interest which they received from money invested in government stocks (Document 37) or in one or other of the many new companies (Document 5).

When prices rose, as the document shows, these people found that they could not manage.

In addition, there was the increase in taxation to pay for the slowly developing welfare state (Document 27). Increased income tax took away more of their income.

# Questions

a. What had happened to the 'great houses' in London?
b. Why had this happened?
c. Who now 'live in a minute flat'?
d. How had prices changed: (i) from 1914 to 1920; (ii) after 1931?
e. What was meant by 'upkeep' in line 4? Why could people living on fixed incomes not manage in the 1920s?
f. Compare the life of the middle and richer people in the 1920s with their life before 1914 (as in Document 21).
g. What evidence is there in this extract that the number of domestic servants was falling? What work were the former servants doing? (See also Document 20.)
h. How does the fall in prices by 1933 help to explain the affluence of Britain shown in Document 24?

# 24 Improved Living Standards, 1920–39

Most remarkable was the looks of women. The prematurely aged wife was coming to be the exception. Children were fewer [Plate 5b], healthier [Plate 12] and gave less trouble; labour-saving devices were introduced, especially for washing, cleaning and cooking — the introduction of stainless cutlery saved an appreciable amount of time; this was only one of a hundred such innovations. Advertising of branded goods was simplifying shopping. Housewives came to count on certain brands of goods; food was sold in the nearest possible stage to table-readiness: the complicated processes of making custard and other puddings were reduced by the use of prepared powders. Cereals, eaten with milk, began to challenge bacon and eggs in prosperous homes, and the bread and margarine of the poor.

Bottled and tinned goods grew more plentiful. The only choice (had been) soup, salmon, corned beef, Californian fruits and potted meat; by the Thirties almost every kind of domestic and foreign fruit, meat, game, fish, vegetable could be bought. Foodstuffs were also gradually standardized: eggs, milk and butter were graded and guaranteed.

Woolworth's stores were the great cheap providers of household utensils and materials. Wherever a new branch was opened, the prices of ironmongers, drapers and household furnishers in the neighbourhood would drop twopence in the shilling. The middle class at first affected to despise Woolworth's, but they soon caught the working-class habit.

Woolworth's, the Building Societies and the Instalment System made it possible for people of small means to take over new houses. The instalment, or 'never-never', system was being applied to all major household purchases, such as furniture, sewing-machines, vacuum-cleaners, gas-ovens, wireless sets.

Robert Graves and Alan Hodge, *The Long Weekend*, 1950.

# Comment

The inter-war period (1919–39) was one in which a large minority were unemployed (Section 7, Document 28). For the majority of the population in the 1920s and 1930s was a period of falling prices and stable wage rates, life was good. Because prices fell people were able to buy more and/or different things, and their standard of living rose. This improvement could be seen in the health of children and the fall in the figures of infant mortality (Document 15).

As the document shows, shopping became better, there were more household goods, life became easier — housekeeping, cooking and meals simpler.

In this extract there is evidence that the social revolution which has taken place since 1945 had its roots in the 1920s and 1930s. In that period many people enjoyed a higher standard of living. In the period since 1945 everyone has enjoyed a higher standard.

# Questions

a. 'the prematurely aged wife was . . . the exception'. How did (i) the children, (ii) household inventions contribute to this improvement?
b. Name three inventions which made (i) washing, (ii) cleaning, (iii) cooking easier. Why did this reduce the need for domestic servants? (Read again Document 21 and think of fires; read also Document 20.)
c. How did (i) advertising, (ii) branded goods simplify shopping?
d. In what ways: (i) was it easier to prepare a meal; (ii) were similar breakfasts being eaten in the homes of 'the prosperous' and 'the poor'?
e. What bottled and tinned goods became available? How does this: (i) help the housewife; (ii) indicate a rising standard of living for many?
f. What goods did Woolworth's supply? Why was this shop welcomed by housewives?
g. What helped 'people of small means to take over new houses'? How did hire purchase help?
h. What evidence is there that the 1930s was a period in which living standards rose? Think of food, shops, household goods. (See also Document 6 and Document 11, Question (g).)

7a. The Jarrow marchers arrive in London.

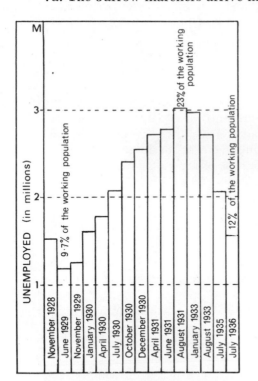

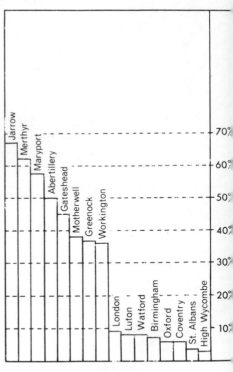

7b. Unemployment figures 1928–36. Unemployment increased as world trade declined. With recovery in trade, the unemployment figures went down. The price of raw materials fell by 56%, and of food by 48%.

7c. The percentage of workers unemployed in various places in 1934. Notice the flight to London and the south, away from the old industrial areas.

# Comment

Plate 7b illustrates the way in which unemployment became a feature of British life in the 1930s. For almost 6 years there were never less than 2 million unemployed; there were in addition many who worked only part-time. Some towns were more affected than others: towns which had depended on coal-mining (Document 7), shipbuilding or cotton (Document 8) had a higher level of unemployment than towns which had a number of industries or towns in which one of the new industries was developing. Plate 7c illustrates this.

For the individual worker there was very little hope. Some left the depressed areas (Document 28) for the South and South-east; others, usually the older people, remained behind. Many towns organised marches of unemployed to London to draw attention to the desperate situation. Plate 7a shows the most famous of these — the Jarrow March of 1936.

# Questions

*a.* What was the level of unemployment in April 1930? In April 1931? When did the level of unemployment start to go down?

*b.* Mark on a map the towns with high levels of unemployment in 1934. Do you know what the main industries of these towns had been?

*c.* Mark on a map the towns which had low levels of unemployment in 1934. How do these figures help you to understand why men left South Wales to look for work?

*d.* Why did the cost of living fall from 1929 to 1933? How did this affect the living standards of those that had work? (See also Document 20.)

*e.* Where have the marchers (Plate 7a) come from? Why did they march to London? How far had they to walk?

# 25 A Visit to a Workhouse, 1892

Going down the narrow lane, waiting while an official looked through a grating and hearing his unpleasant voice, made me understand why the poor dreaded these places. I realised how all these prison sort of surroundings were making decent people endure any suffering rather than enter. Officials, whitewashed walls, huge books for name, history, searching, being stripped and bathed in a communal tub, and being dressed in clothes which had been worn by lots of other people — everything possible was done to inflict degradation.

Officers looked upon these people as a nuisance. Clothing was of the usual workhouse type. No undergarments for men or women, boots worn till they fell off. The paupers were allowed out once a month and could be visited once a month. Men were put to stone-breaking or oakum picking. No effort was made to find work for men or women.

On one visit I inspected the supper of oatmeal porridge, with pieces of black stuff floating around. We discovered it to be rat and mice manure. I called for the chief officer, who said the porridge was good and wholesome. 'Very good, madam,' said I, 'here you are, eat one mouthful.' 'Oh dear, no,' said the fine lady, 'the food is not for me, and is good and wholesome enough for those who want it.' I stamped and shouted around till both doctor and master arrived, both of whom pleaded it was all a mistake, and promptly served cocoa and bread and margarine.

George Lansbury, *My Life*, 1931.

# Comment

A major change in the administration of the Poor Law came in 1894 when the new Local Government Act allowed women and working men to become candidates for election to the Boards of Guardians. One such man was George Lansbury, the author of this extract. He became a Guardian of the Poor in Poplar, a dockside parish of East London, and visited the local workhouse.

The standard of 'less eligibility' is well illustrated here in regard to clothing and food. The attitude of the officials towards the poor may not have been typical, but the effect of living in such an institution can only have degraded.

# Questions

*a.* Why does Lansbury speak of 'prison . . . surroundings'?
*b.* How were the poor treated on their arrival at the workhouse?
*c.* Why did 'decent people endure any suffering rather than enter' the workhouse?
*d.* How were the inhabitants dressed?
*e.* What has Lansbury to say about the possibilities of the paupers meeting their relatives and friends?
*f.* Why did Lansbury 'stamp and shout'? Why did the inmates not do so?
*g.* Why would working-class Guardians tend to have more sympathy with the inmates of the workhouse than the middle classes?
*h.* What 'work' did the paupers perform?

# 26 The Existence Level, 1900

The wage for a labourer in York is from 18*s*. to 21*s*.; the minimum expenditure necessary to maintain in a state of physical efficiency a family of two adults and three children is 21*s*. 8*d*., or, if there are four children, 26*s*.

The wages paid for unskilled labour in York are insufficient to provide food, shelter and clothing adequate to maintain in a state of bare physical efficiency, even if the diet is less generous than that allowed in the Workhouse.

And let us clearly understand what 'merely physical efficiency' means. A family living upon the scale allowed for in this estimate must never spend a penny on railway or omnibus; never go into the country unless they walk; never purchase a halfpenny newspaper or buy a ticket for a popular concert; never write letters to absent children, for they cannot afford the postage. They cannot save, join sick club or Trade Union; they cannot pay the subscriptions. The children have no pocket money for dolls, marbles, or sweets. The father must not smoke or drink. The mother must never buy any pretty clothes for herself or for her children. 'Nothing must be bought but that which is absolutely necessary for the maintenance of physical health, and what is bought must be of the plainest and most economical description.' Finally, the wage-earner must never be absent from his work for a single day.

If any of these conditions are broken, the extra expenditure is met, and can only be met, by limiting the diet; or in other words by sacrificing physical efficiency.

B. Seebohm Rowntree, *Poverty: A Study in Town Life*, 1902.

# Comment

This extract is from *Poverty*, the analysis and description by Seebohm Rowntree of poverty in York. Having read Booth's work on poverty in London, Rowntree took two years to complete the examination of conditions in York, and his analysis served as a model for future investigation. His findings, the result of thorough investigation, were as startling as were those of Booth. He found that 43·4% of the working classes, representing 27·84% of the population of York, were living in poverty. Some 10% of the population lived in abject poverty, in which the total family earnings were insufficient to obtain the minimum necessities for the maintenance of even physical efficiency; the other 17% lived in secondary poverty, in which the total family earnings were barely sufficient for the maintenance of physical efficiency.

# Questions

*a.* What was the average wage for a labourer in York?
*b.* Why were the families of such labourers unable to 'maintain . . .
  physical efficiency'?
*c.* What sort of diet is included in the estimates of 'physical efficiency'?
  Read the list of things on which they must 'never spend a penny'.
*d.* How would this affect their use of leisure time? (See Document 10
  and Plate 3.)
*e.* Why could they not join any insurance schemes? (See Document 27
  and Book I, Document 32.)
*f.* How were (i) children, (ii) mothers affected?
*g.* Why was it unlikely that even this low wage could be guaranteed?
  ('. . . for a single day'.)
*h.* How does this extract explain: (i) the appearance of the children in
  Plate 12a; (ii) infant mortality figures (Document 15); (iii) the
  improvements seen by Eleanor Rathbone between 1914 and 1918
  (Document 16)?

# 27 Lloyd George on National Insurance, 1911

What is the explanation that only a portion of the working classes have made provision against sickness and unemployment? Because very few can afford to pay the premiums at a rate of 1s. 6d. or 2s. per week at the very lowest. There are a multitude of the working classes who cannot spare that, because it involves the deprivation of children of the necessaries of life. Therefore the vast majority choose to insure against death alone. Those who can afford to take up two policies insure against death and sickness, and those who can afford to take up three insure against death, sickness and unemployment, but only in that order. Why not insure against all three? Their wages are too low to enable them to insure against all three. The second difficulty is that during a period of sickness or unemployment, when they are earning nothing, they cannot keep up the premiums, so, in circumstances over which they have no control, (they) abandon their policies. That is the reason why not one half of the workmen have made any provision for sickness and not one-tenth for unemployment. There is a real need for some system which would aid the workmen over these difficulties. A system of national insurance which would invoke the aid of the State and of the employer to enable the workman to get over these difficulties and make provision for himself for sickness, and, as far as the most precarious trades are concerned, against unemployment.

*Parliamentary Debates*, 5th Series, vol. 25.

# Comment

The causes of poverty were known (Document 26). The passing of the Industrial Liability Acts (1894 and 1897), the Old Age Pensions Act (1908), Trades Boards Act (1909) and the Unemployed Workmen's Act (1905) are stages along the road towards a welfare state. This extract is from Lloyd George's speech introducing a bill to provide health insurance. It illustrates another step along that road.

Increased taxation follows. In 1870 public expenditure (in rates and taxes) on social services was 6s. 3d. per year per head of the population. In 1910 it was £1 0s. 9d. and in 1920 £1 9s. 5d. The taxpayer paid, on average, 3d. per head in 1870, 7d. in 1910 and 8d. in 1920.

# Questions

a. Lloyd George asked a question in line 1, and provided the answer. Does your reading of Documents 22 and 26 help you to agree with his answer?
b. What is a premium? How much would an insurance company charge for a policy 'against sickness and unemployment'?
c. In what order did working men take out insurance policies?
d. Why were they often forced to 'abandon their policies'?
e. How did Lloyd George propose to overcome 'these difficulties'?
f. Why would 'the aid of the State' require increased taxation? (See again Document 16, Question (h).)
g. Write a paragraph on the 1911 National Insurance Act, Part 1. Show: (i) who paid into the Fund; (ii) what workers could join the scheme; (iii) what benefit they derived from it.
h. Write a paragraph on Part 2 of the 1911 National Insurance Act.

# 28 Men Without Work, 1938

Where the wife was earning but the husband unemployed, there was evidently unhappiness. A printer, 42 years old, who had lost his chance of re-employment at his old trade, had left Liverpool in the hopes of finding work in the Midlands; the wife showed us a touching letter in which he told her that he had got work at 25*s*. a week and enclosed 10*s*. for her. She had been working, so he only drew 5*s*. Unemployment Assistance. She used to hear him 'tramping up and down the garden path, or up and down in the parlour, and it made her nearly mad, and it made her nearly mad to feel that she was keeping him by her earnings and they gaining nothing by her work'.

There is the man whose allowance takes into account the fact that his children are earning. There were men over 55 years of age who were either not in receipt of any Unemployment Assistance or in receipt of small amounts, 5*s*. or 7*s*. 6*d*., because it was held that the household resources were otherwise sufficient. Some men feel the loss of an independent income they enjoyed while on Unemployment Benefit, and the home appears to represent two standards, the earning children being often smartly dressed and happy, the fathers shabby and suffering from a sense of their dependence. They purposely avoided making any effort to keep up appearances in case the children might think that they were drawing an undue share of the family income.

*Pilgrim Trust Report*, 1938.

## Comment

Unemployment was not just a matter of statistics, although statistics are important. It was a personal matter for each person unemployed. Some were out of work for a few weeks only; some, younger, people had never had a job after leaving school; some, older, had been out of work for months or years. The sight of these men caused George Orwell to write *The Road to Wigan Pier*, and made younger intellectuals critical of the economic system.

7d. Unemployed man
in Wigan, 1939.

The Pilgrim Trust set up a Committee under Archbishop Temple to examine the psychological effects of unemployment. This document is an extract from the report of this Committee (1938).

## Questions

*a.* Where had the unemployed husband: (i) lived; (ii) gone to look for a job?

*b.* What was his wage in 1935? Documents 22, 26 and 27 tell us something about working-class life in the beginning of the century. How far was this still a true picture of working-class life?

*c.* What was: (i) Unemployment Benefit; (ii) Unemployment Assistance?

*d.* Why did the wife say that 'he *only* drew 5s. Unemployment Assistance'?

*e.* In what way were 'they gaining nothing by her work'?

*f.* Give two reasons why a man's Assistance might be reduced.

*g.* How had this affected many fathers of working children?

*h.* Read Document 20 again. Why was the wife in Document 28 able to find a job? What does this tell us of: (i) the need for retraining workmen; (ii) the increased opportunities for women to find work?

# Comment

The General Strike (Document 32) meant an almost complete stoppage of work. The Government had organised a system of food distribution, using the Army and Navy; many volunteers came forward to drive buses, lorries, trams and railway trains. As the plates show, these volunteers were protected by the police; the authorities expected trouble. In Plymouth the police and strikers organised a football match to raise money; in many places canteens, set up to feed volunteer workers, also fed the strike-pickets. The Russian Communists despaired; the British workman was not a revolutionary.

# Questions

*a.* What evidence is there in the plates that many people came out on strike?
*b.* How do the plates indicate that the Government expected clashes between the strikers and the volunteers?
*c.* What evidence is there that the police did not come out on strike?
*d.* What effect did the strike have on shopkeepers?
*e.* Who is guarding the bus driver? Why?

8a. The General Strike, 1926. A policeman sits on the bonnet of a bus driven by a volunteer, to prevent an attack by strikers.

8b. The great food convoy of 8th May 1926. It went from East India Docks to the Hyde Park food depots.

# 29 The Dockers' Strike, 1889

The dock labourers and their allies have won a remarkable victory. The dock companies have granted all their demands . . . the strike will remain a most significant event in the relations between capital and labour. There is first the fact that the dock labourers, possessed of no special skill, industry or strength, have been able to combine — combination hitherto having been considered a weapon only available for the skilled labourer. But this was by no means the most remarkable phenomenon of the strike. The hard case of the men elicited the sympathy of all the various categories of riverside labourers without exception. These made up a compact industry army, without whom the shipping trade of London could not proceed; and it accordingly stood still. The case of the dock labourers took a powerful hold upon public opinion. It drew sympathy and material support from all quarters; for some yet unexplained reason, from Australia above all. Thus the men were placed beyond the reach of starvation. They were enabled to bargain on equal terms with their employers; and they were eventually successful. The hints afforded by the great strike will probably not be neglected in the future. It would not be too much to say that we may look for a large development of them in future conflicts between capital and labour. The alliance of riverside labourers, possessing various grades of skill and social standing, will probably be taken as an encouragement to carry into effect wider federations of labour.

*The Times*, 16th September 1889.

# Comment

Model unions were formed among the skilled workers. The benefits that these enjoyed from high wages and strong unions were reflected in their relatively high standard of living. In the 1880s unions were formed for the first time for the unskilled and casual workmen.

The first of these (formed by Annie Besant) was a union for the girls at Bryant and May's match factory. Another, formed by Will Thorne, was for the gas workers. The most important was the London Dock Labourers' Union. The members paid a 1d. per week to their union, and received no social benefits (see Book I, Document 32). They possessed no special skills and so could easily be replaced.

The London Dockers' Strike was a significant development. The workpeople learned the value of united action. They found leadership and organisation that they had not known they possessed.

# Questions

*a.* Why was it significant that the dock labourers 'have been able to combine'? Who had formed unions before this?

*b.* The dock labourers went on strike. Who supported them? Why did they make 'a compact army'?

*c.* What effect had the strike had on public opinion? Compare this with the former attitude towards trade unions. (See Book I, Documents 29–32.)

*d.* Why were the men saved from starvation? Why was this important?

*e.* What does the writer think will happen in 'future conflicts'? How would this affect: (i) the size; (ii) the number of trade unions?

*f.* This strike took place in 1889. When did the working classes gain the vote? When was the Labour Party formed? (See Document 41.)

*g.* The dockers were 'unskilled'. Read Documents 22, 26 and 27 again. Why did the unskilled labourer need state welfare services more than did the skilled workman? (See Book I, Document 32.)

*h.* Find out the dates for: (i) the founding of the Agricultural Workers' Union by Joseph Arch; (ii) the strike of match girls at Bryant & May's. How do these events and the Dockers' Strike indicate a growing militancy on the part of some of the lower classes?

# 30 The Taff Vale Decision, 1901

The judgement makes no change in the lawfulness of Trade Unionism. No act is made wrongful which was not wrongful before. If a Trade Union causes damage, it seems fair that it should be liable for what it has done. The grievance of the Trade Unions lies in the uncertainty of the English law, and its liability to be used as a means of oppression. This is increased by the dislike of Trade Unionism which nearly all judges and juries share with the rest of the upper and middle classes.

The middle classes are more hostile to Trade Unionism than a generation ago. In 1867–75, when Trade Unionism was struggling for legal recognition, it seemed only fair that the workmen should be put in a position to make a good fight of it against the employers. Accordingly, combinations, strikes and peaceful picketing were legalised . . . It all belonged to the conception of a labor dispute as a fight between the parties, in which the State could do no more than keep the ring. Gradually this has given way to the view that the stoppage of work by an industrial dispute is a public nuisance, which ought to be prevented by the Government. Public opinion has become uneasy about the capacity of English manufacturers to hold their own against foreign competition, and therefore resents any attempt to restrict output or obstruct machinery, of which the Trade Unions may be accused.

S. and B. Webb, *Industrial Democracy*, 1902.

# Comment

The Taff Vale strike began as an unofficial strike in August 1900. The Amalgamated Society of Railway Servants (later the National Union of Railwaymen) made the strike official. Acts of sabotage by strikers caused damage to the property of the Taff Vale Railway Company. The Company sued the union for the amount of damages, and the Law Lords decided that the union would have to pay £23,000 in damages and £27,000 in costs.

The effects of this decision was that unions would not be willing to call strikes in the future, for fear of being sued for damages. This meant that trade unions would be in a weak position when it came to bargaining with employers, because they would be unwilling to use the strike weapon.

The Government might have won the support of trade unionists. The Balfour Government did nothing. The unions then turned to the smaller Labour Party (Document 41), which had been formed by the unskilled unions and the various socialist parties (Document 41). The skilled unions (bigger and with more money) had remained outside this party. The Taff Vale decision drove these unions into the Labour Party.

# Questions

a. What had 'the judgement' said?
b. How might this be used 'as a means of oppression' against trade unions?
c. Why was this likely, according to the Webbs?
d. Why had the middle classes been favourable to trade unions 'a generation ago'?
e. What laws were passed to help trade unions in 1867–75? Why has 'public opinion become uneasy' about trade unions?
f. What was the Taff Vale dispute about?
g. What Act was passed in 1906 to restore the legal position of trade unions?
h. Unskilled workers were the first to form a political party (Documents 29 and 41). Why did the Taff Vale judgement make skilled unions take a more active interest in politics?

# 31 The Triple Alliance, 1914

One result of the industrial unrest of recent years is the Triple Industrial Alliance.

At the Miners' Annual Conference in 1913, a resolution was passed, 'That the Executive Committee of the Miners' Federation approach the Executive Committees of other big Trade Unions with a view to co-operative action.'

The miners had a joint meeting with the representatives of the two industries most comparable to their own — railways and transport.

The three bodies have much in common. Their membership is considerable, the miners numbering 800,000, the railwaymen 270,000 and the transport workers 250,000. The miners have done much fighting; the railwaymen have come through struggles similar to our own; and the transport workers are famed for their fighting spirit and fighting qualities. But a great deal of suffering and privation has been caused. A strike on the railway system affects the miners and the transport workers. When the miners struck in 1912 the cost to the railwaymen alone was about £94,000.

The new body is not to be a rival to any other. Nor is it to be sectional in any sense. There is no suggestion that if one section of the miners determines to strike they will receive the assistance of the new alliance. Action is to be confined to joint national action. The predominant idea is that each of these great fighting organisations, before embarking upon any big movement, either defensive or aggressive, should formulate its programme, submit it to the others, and that upon joint proposals action should then be taken.

It will be wise, indeed essential, to have the working agreement ready for the days of peace after the war. It is then that we may expect an attack on Labour by the employers.

Robert Smillie, *The Labour Year Book*, 1916.

# Comment

The growth of larger firms was a feature of industrial development after 1870 (see Document 5). In this extract Robert Smillie, President of the Miners' Federation (1912–21), explains why the larger unions felt it necessary to work together. In this extract we can see some of the reasons for the General Strike (Document 32).

# Questions

a. Which unions formed the Triple Industrial Alliance? What had helped the formation of large, *national* unions?
b. What did the Miners' Federation hope for in 1913?
c. What two things did these three unions have in common?
d. How did a strike on the railways affect the miners and the transport workers? Why?
e. Would (i) an unofficial strike or (ii) a local dispute lead to immediate action by the Triple Alliance?
f. How would the Alliance ensure that only united action took place?
g. How does this document help you to understand the calling of the General Strike? (See Document 32.)
h. Look up the terms of the Trade Union Act, 1927. How did this Act affect the Triple Alliance?

# 32 The General Strike, 1926

On Friday, April 30th, we went to the House of Commons waiting for the Prime Minister to come from Downing Street. We never left the room at the House of Commons except to have some light refreshments, while the Prime Minister was meeting the owners. It was nearly seven o'clock by the time we got down to discussions. Hardly had we done so when Thomas produced a poster, announcing that the Government had proclaimed an emergency. It gave us an insight into the Government's determination to face a national stoppage. Jimmy Thomas asked [him] had this poster been ordered by the Government. Baldwin flushed. Everyone of us concluded that we had been badly tricked. We felt we could no longer trust Baldwin, and that they were simply playing for time to complete the arrangements which they had in hand. I told the Prime Minister that we had been relying on his assurance of good faith.

The atmosphere was tense indeed, and Thomas followed me with the gravest warnings to the Government. He concluded: 'I picture it as a whirlpool, knowing I cannot help being dragged in, knowing that the State must win on an issue like this. I believe that nothing which my colleagues or myself can do will prevent that plunge with the consequences that I believe are inevitable.'

It was a dramatic statement and not without its effects on Baldwin. The Government then put to us questions regarding the possibility of considering a wage reduction, but we refused to countenance this, and we said we would retire to consult the miners. We returned again to meet the Prime Minister at 9.45 p.m. Churchill met Thomas outside the Prime Minister's room for a casual moment, and asked: 'Is it over?' Thomas said, 'Yes.' Churchill replied, 'Well, it is over as far as we are concerned. I have given you twenty-four millions, and that is all you are going to get. You can't have another bob.'

Lord Citrine, *Men and Work*, 1964.

# Comment

This is an extract from the autobiography of Sir Walter Citrine, who was a member of the Industrial Committee set up by the General Council of the Trade Union Congress to negotiate with the Government and the mine-owners in 1926.

The coal industry was no longer prosperous (Document 7). The return to the Gold Standard (Document 4) had made matters worse. The owners had wanted to cut wages in 1925; threats of a General Strike had forced the Government to pay a subsidy to the industry while a Royal Commission looked into the industry.

This (Samuel) Commission made a number of recommendations for improving the industry; these were rejected by the owners. The Commission also recommended a cut in miners' wages; this was rejected by their union, which was supported by the union movement as a whole. (See Document 31.)

The negotiations failed and the General Strike of 1926 followed.

# Questions

*a.* Why did the owners seek, and the Samuel Commission recommend, a cut in wages? (See Document 4, Question (*f*).)
*b.* What office did Mr. Churchill hold at this time?
*c.* What did the 'poster' proclaim? Why did this poster upset the union leaders?
*d.* What evidence is there that Jimmy Thomas did not expect the strike to succeed?
*e.* Why were the union leaders unwilling to consider a wage reduction for the miners (Document 31)?
*f.* What did Mr. Churchill mean by 'I have given you twenty-four millions'?
*g.* When did the General Strike begin? How long did it last? Which union remained out on strike?

# THE DAWN OF HOPE.

Mr. LLOYD GEORGE'S National Health Insurance Bill provides for the insurance of the Worker in case of Sickness.

**Support the Liberal Government**
in their policy of
**SOCIAL REFORM.**

9b.

# Comment

The period 1870–1939 saw an increase in the activity of both central and local governments. Some older ministries were given increased powers; some new ministries were formed to deal with the new laws. Each ministry required Civil Servants; these required offices in which to work. This plate gives some idea of the growth of the Civil Service and of increased government activity.

# Questions

a. Why were many government offices required in Victoria's reign?
b. What suggests that there were a large number of people working in these offices?
c. What suggests that the work done in these buildings was clean? Why did this mean that respectable women had increased opportunities for work?
d. These offices are in London? Why?
e. Notice the carriages in Plate 9a. What inventions (transport and communications) made it easier for a Government to see that laws were applied over the whole country?

9a. The new façade of the Privy Council Office, designed by Barry. This is only one of the government offices which transformed the appearance of Whitehall and Parliament Street.

# 33 What Civil Equality Means

The same observations apply to the question of civil equality. It will never be established so long as you have five hundred men nominated by the lottery of birth thwarting the wishes of the majority of their countrymen in the determination of the best way of governing.

New Liberalism devotes its endeavour to removing the causes of discontent. Men cannot live by bread alone; (but) a man cannot live without bread . . . Poverty is the result of a man's own misconduct or of misfortune. In so far as he brings it on himself, the State cannot accomplish much. In so far as poverty is due to circumstances over which the man has no control, then the State should step in and save the man from the physical and mental torture involved in extreme penury . . . The aged we have dealt with during the present Session. We are still confronted with the more gigantic task of dealing with the rest — the sick, the infirm, the unemployed, the widows and the orphans. Is it just, or humane, to let them suffer privation? I do not think the better-off classes, whose comfort is assured, realise the sufferings of the unemployed man who does not know how long he can keep a roof over his head, and where he will turn to find a meal for the pinched and hungry little children who look to him for sustenance and protection. This is what unemployment means.

D. Lloyd George, in a speech at Swansea, 1st October 1908.

# Comment

Gladstonian Liberalism, concerned for the individual and his freedom, regarded government activity as interference with the individual's freedom. It failed to see that 'freedom' was, for many, a meaningless word unless the means to be free were provided.

The new Liberalism aimed at carrying out a programme of social reform. Lloyd George was the leader here, and illustrates the changing nature of the Liberal Party. Lloyd George, brought up in relative poverty by an uncle who was a cobbler, articled as a clerk to a small town solicitor, and self-educated, was nearer to the people than were the older Liberal leaders.

He appreciated the real meaning of freedom and the desire of the newly enfranchised voters for a greater share in the country's prosperity.

# Questions

a. '. . . five hundred . . . birth'. Of whom is Lloyd George speaking? (See also Plate 11.)

b. How could these men thwart 'the wishes of the majority of their countrymen'?

c. Why does Lloyd George speak of 'New Liberalism'? How does it differ from 'Old Liberalism'?

d. What were the causes of poverty? When could the State not 'accomplish much'?

e. How do Documents 22, 26 and 28 support the view that sometimes 'poverty is due to circumstances over which the man has no control'?

f. What six groups were poor, according to Lloyd George. Which one had the Liberals 'dealt with'?

g. How did Lloyd George describe unemployment?

h. List five major Acts passed before 1906 and 1913 to improve social conditions.

# 34 A Possible Cure for Unemployment, 1930

New capital investment at home would create additional employment. In addition to the men directly employed and to the men occupied in making and transporting the materials required, there will be a further set of men put into work to supply the needs created by the additional purchasing power of the first set of men.

We may illustrate our argument briefly:

(i) A considerable part of the larger towns of the country need rebuilding on a comprehensive scale. At present they offer neither beauty nor convenience nor health. Much of the housing of the country is only fit to be demolished. It seems an insanity to keep a large proportion of the building trade out of employment when this is the case.

(ii) Some of our staple industries need to be refitted on modern lines, a substantial capital expenditure. In several cases, there is much to be said for replanning an industry as a whole. Why should our staple industries wait? We think that a body should be set up (the Board of National Investment) in the hands of which all matters relating to schemes of long-term national investment would be concentrated. This Board might be entrusted with the duty of raising funds for the local authorities including municipalities, for the telephones, for the roads and for such further schemes of national development as those which we have suggested above.

*Minority Report of the Macmillan Committee*, 1930–1, Parliamentary Papers, Cmd. 3897.

# Comment

The Macmillan Committee was appointed by the Labour Government (1929–31) to enquire into certain aspects of financial policy. J. M. Keynes, a member of the Liberal Party and an eminent economist, was a member of the Committee who criticised the ideas and policies of Montagu Norman (Document 4) pointing to their harmful effects. This extract is part of a Minority Report by Keynes and others.

Investment of money is needed for the building of houses, roads, bridges, schools, railways, power stations, factories, machinery, ships, etc. Keynes argued that if there were more investments at home many more people would find work. He gives examples of what might be done.

The 'cost' of investment is the rate of interest paid for the money borrowed (Document 4). When the Bank Rate is high there is less borrowing; Keynes wanted a low Bank Rate which would encourage borrowing. When the Bank Rate fell after 1931 there was a huge increase in the amount of private house building.

# Questions

a. 'New capital investment at home'. What investment did Keynes suggest in (i) and (ii)? (One line answers only.)
b. '. . . towns need rebuilding . . .' Name five trades which would have been 'directly employed'.
c. Why would this direct employment lead to employment for a 'further set of men'?
d. Look again at Plate 4. How, according to Keynes, could slum-clearance help: (i) cure unemployment; (ii) improve the nation's health?
e. Read again Document 14. Why would slum-clearance require increased activity by the central and local governments?
f. Which industries needed 'to be refitted'? (See also Documents 2, 7 and 8.) How would this refitting help cure unemployment?
g. What work would the Board of National Investment perform?
h. Why would building a ship at Jarrow (Plate 7) mean work for: (i) coal-miners; (ii) steel workers; (iii) transport workers?

# 35 Central and Local Governments Unite in Action, 1930s

Since Sir Richard Cross's Act of 1875, which first enabled local authorities to deal with congested areas, down to 1930 about 178,000 persons living in slum dwellings had been rehoused. The Slum Clearance Act of 1930 had added about 20,000 more, but the response of the local authorities had been disappointing.

Why had progress been so slow? Of all tasks in the field of housing slum clearance was the most difficult. It could only be tackled by the local authorities, but the cost of the undertaking and the slum owners' opposition made even progressive authorities reluctant. It was so much easier to build new estates in the hope that slum dwellers would get a chance of moving into them.

In the January recess of 1933 I went on a three weeks' slum tour through the North of England. Our programme was the same in each town. The Mayor and the Housing Committee conducted us on a tour of the worst housing areas. We did our job thoroughly from morning to night and inspected areas of tens of thousands of houses which had been condemned and recondemned for a generation as unfit for human habitation. Instead of the normal density of 12 houses to the acre on council estates, densities of 60 to 70 per acre were quite common. These slum hovels were, of course, a profitable investment.

I went back to the Ministry like a man possessed and my anger maintained a white-hot heat which carried me through the ardours of the campaign.

On April 6th, 1933, a strongly worded circular went out to 1,700 local authorities. An imperative request was made for a concerted effort against slums. 'The Minister', the circular concluded, 'will be glad to receive a copy of the programme adopted by the local authority.'

Sir Geoffrey Shakespeare, *Let Candles be Brought In*, 1949.

# Comment

This is an extract from the memoirs of Sir Geoffrey Shakespeare, who was Parliamentary Secretary to the Minister of Health in the National Government formed in 1931 (see Document 43). The Ministry of Health (see also Document 15) was responsible for the slum-clearance campaign (see also Document 14). This extract shows that the solution to this social problem required: (i) laws passed by the central government; (ii) active local authorities which would use the powers given them; (iii) increased expenditure by both central and local governments. (See also Document 36.)

# Questions

*a.* Read Documents 28 and 34. How might a slum-clearance campaign have helped to lower the level of unemployment?
*b.* What Acts of Parliament are mentioned in this extract? How does this help you to understand that the creation of the Welfare State is not the work of one political party?
*c.* How many slum-dwellers had been rehoused between 1875 and 1930? How many had been rehoused after the Greenwood Slum Clearance Act of 1930?
*d.* Why were the slum-dwellers unable to afford the rents of the houses on the new council estates? (See Documents 26 and 28.)
*e.* Draw a 1″ square and on it make 12 marks representing the 'normal density'. On another 1″ square make 60 marks to represent slum densities.
*f.* Why would slum-clearance lead to the outward spread of towns?
*g.* Show how (i) the central government (Acts of Parliament, subsidies and circular) and (ii) the local authorities, co-operated in this campaign.
*h.* Why did this campaign lead to: (i) increased taxation; (ii) less infant mortality? (See also Document 15 and Plate 4.)

# 36 The Civil Service and the National Insurance Act

Recruitment was now by open competitive examination. 1,000 administrative officers were recruited at the age of about twenty-two by a competitive examination, deliberately related to the final honours schools of the Universities.

The examination itself was arduous and exacting but was successful in selecting the best 40 or so out of 400. Basil Blackett and John Anderson were actually first on their respective lists, and twenty years later they would have been pronounced the best of their years.

The tasks of the Civil Service were more restricted than they are now, because the State confined itself to such functions as the insistence on safety precautions in mines and factories.

Very soon Lloyd George was putting his National Health Insurance Bill through Parliament. The new Bill would involve central administration on a scale hitherto unknown. A small staff only was required immediately but it would become the nucleus of a large office a little later.

The technical work on (the Bill) was handled by a small band under the lead of a remarkable civil servant, W. J. Braithwaite. The Government chose as Chairman of the English Commission, Sir Robert Morant, the most remarkable civil servant of his day. He had been largely responsible for a transformation of the educational system; and was at the same time intensely interested in medical research and organisation.

It was a revealing experience to see what a Department so led could do when entrusted with a vast and constructive job; and the way in which, with the aid of so many drawn from other Departments, the whole Government Service could be used as a single instrument for the most urgent task of the moment.

Lord Salter, *Memoirs of a Public Servant*, 1961.

# Comment

Lord Salter, the author of *Memoirs of a Public Servant*, entered the Civil Service in 1904 and resigned in 1931. He joined a reformed Civil Service. The 'old' Civil Service had allowed Ministers and higher Civil Servants to appoint new Civil Servants, a system which had a good deal of corruption and favouritism. Equality of opportunity was now demanded for the Civil Service. The examination system resulted and its success is shown in the extract.

# Questions

*a.* How were Civil Servants 'recruited'? Why was this welcomed by clever boys and girls?

*b.* How were 'administrative officers' recruited? Did Lord Salter think that the system produced good results?

*c.* Why did the growth of the Civil Service result in an increased demand for higher education?

*d.* 'The tasks of the Civil Service'. How do Documents 14, 15, 16, 27 and 28 help to explain the increase in the size of the Civil Service?

*e.* What does Lord Salter say about Robert Morant? (See also Document 46.)

*f.* How did the National Health Insurance Bill affect the size of the Civil Service: (i) immediately; (ii) '. . . a little later'?

*g.* How did the increase in the size of the Civil Service provide opportunities for women to find work (Document 20)?

*h.* Why would Keynes's ideas (Document 34) have led to an enlarged Civil Service?

# Comment

The British farmer was the first to feel the effects of international competition (Document 1). Plate 10a shows the unloading of American wheat in the Port of London. Notice the three methods of driving a vessel — the oarsman, the sail and the steam engine. The caption tells the rest of the story.

# Questions

*a.* Why did the price of transporting grain fall after 1868?

*b.* What evidence is there in the plate of changes in the shipping industry?

*c.* A great deal was imported; 'the British housewife . . . the target of producers'. What does this tell you of the wealth of the British at the end of the 19th century?

*d.* Prices fell. What effect did this have on the standard of living of the townsfolk?

*e.* Who suffered as a result of this increased importing of cheap food?

10a. An American grain elevator used for unloading wheat ships at London docks during the 1870s.

10b. British farming was more primitive. Here is a man filling a water cart, about 1887.

# 37 British Capital Going Abroad

British capital flowed into Canada, the United States, Argentina, and other countries in South America also benefited by British investments. British capital poured into South Africa, Egypt, and the colonies on the east and west coasts of Africa were not neglected. India and the Far East vied with Russia and Australia in their endeavours to obtain British capital. The efflux of British capital increased during the years 1904–7. During 1907 the outflow reached £140,000,000, which far exceeds the amount invested in the great boom in 1872. In 1908 and 1909 the outflow of capital showed some decline; in these years the amount appears to have exceeded £100,000,000 per annum. In the three following years the outflow grew again, and appears to have reached further new records.

The main purpose for which these sums are required is railway construction. Docks, water and gas works, electric lighting, telegraphs and tramways, form another important group of enterprises which are constantly demanding fresh capital. All of these activities are conducted both by Governmental authorities and by joint-stock companies. There are mining concerns and plantations and trading companies, which figured prominently during earlier periods of foreign investment. There is a new characteristic of foreign investment during the past few years, namely, a tendency to invest in manufacturing and industrial concerns. The movement is particularly noteworthy in North America, in India and in Russia.

C. K. Hobson, *The Export of Capital*, 1914.

# Comment

The author of this document, C. K. Hobson, explained and analysed the loans to government and industries abroad, a subject which was widely discussed in the early years of this century.

Foreign undeveloped countries could not finance their own industrial revolutions. Britain, as the richest nation in the world, a legacy of our early start and dominance, could provide this money; British industry could sell much of the material required for industrial development; and British craftsmen supplied the required skills. So a foreign government or private company would borrow money on the London Exchange, spend most of it (about 67%) in buying British equipment, pay more of it to British workmen and would then have a harbour, railway, textile mill, etc. (Document 8).

British industries, especially steel, coal and engineering, flourished; so did the country concerned whose farmers and industries became more productive, with effects already seen. The British National Balance Sheet showed (and still shows) profit from this investment overseas in the form of invisible exports of interest and capital repayments.

# Questions

a. List the countries which borrowed money from British investors.
b. When was there a 'great boom'? How much had been invested in: 1907; 1908; 1909?
c. What are the 'main purposes' for which these sums 'are required'?
d. How did building a railway in South America help to provide employment in the British (i) coal, (ii) steel, (iii) engineering industries?
e. What other 'important group of enterprises' borrowed British capital?
f. Who 'conducted' these activities? Why should foreign governments have been anxious to help in their countries' industrial development? (See Documents 2 and 3.)
g. What new 'characteristic of foreign investment' had become evident in 'the past four years'? (See Document 8 on the textile industry.)
h. You have seen why foreign countries wanted to borrow (Questions (c), (e), (f), (g)). Why did they borrow from *British* investors? What does this tell you about the wealth of Britain compared to that of other countries (Document 21)?

# 38 Joseph Chamberlain's *Tariff Reform Campaign,* 20th January 1904

What are the arguments that I have advanced elsewhere? 50 years ago we altered our policy, to secure free exchange with all nations. But we do not (have it). We have free imports instead. Under this system competition with our manufactures has increased. Meanwhile, the prosperity of other countries has increased more rapidly than ours and we are losing our position in the world.

There has been a decrease in the exports of our goods to protected countries. Their policy is to shut out *all* which they think themselves able to produce. That is the object of their protective tariff. I do not say that they close their markets entirely. No, they are wiser than that. They are ready to take our coal . . . (which they cannot produce).

In our own colonies, there is a growth of foreign importation which greatly exceeds the growth of the exportation from the home country. We are not even safe in our own Empire.

In order to maintain our position as a manufacturing nation we must increase our Imperial trade.

It is our duty to put ourselves into a position in which we can bargain with (protected) countries on equal terms.

During the year 1903, the number of people unemployed has risen by 40%. Is that a sign of prosperity? Competition from abroad has grown more and more severe. Wages have been reduced. Almost daily some trade has to submit to a reduction. This is not a proof of prosperity.

(Our opponents) try to frighten you by saying 'You will lose your foreign trade'. Well, has this been the result of the adoption of tariffs by other countries? Following on the adoption of a tariff which has made the home trade secure there has been a great increase in foreign trade also.

*The Times*, 21st January 1904.

# Comment

Joseph Chamberlain was Colonial Secretary in the Conservative and Unionist Government until 1903. Worried by the growth of German industrial power (Document 3) and by the growth of unemployment in Britain (Document 27), Chamberlain was anxious that Britain should abandon Free Trade. He agreed that this had once been advantageous to Britain (Book I, Section 10), but argued that it was no longer so.

This is an extract from a speech made in the Guildhall, London, on 20th January 1904. He had an audience of 4,000, not all of them believers in his ideas. It was the last speech in a campaign which had begun in October 1903, during which he had spoken in many towns and cities throughout the country. His campaign failed to convince the majority of the Tory Party, which went into the election of 1906 split on this issue. He also failed to convince the majority of the electors who voted for the Free Trade Liberals. (See also Document 2.)

# Questions

*a.* What did Chamberlain mean by 'altered our policy'?

*b.* Why did he say that we did not have 'free exchange with all nations'?

*c.* Which countries had caused us to lose 'our position in the world'?

*d.* What reasons, other than Free Trade, can you offer for the success of these countries? (See Documents 1–4, 8 and 37.)

*e.* Why had exports fallen: (i) to 'protected countries'; (ii) 'to our own colonies'?

*f.* What was the effect of this fall in exports on: (i) wage rates; (ii) the level of employment; (iii) profits?

*g.* Had foreign countries suffered after adopting a tariff system?

*h.* What was the effect of the Chamberlain campaign on: (i) the unity of the Conservative Party; (ii) the election of 1906?

# 39 Imperial Preference

The Imperial Conference met in the autumn of 1923. The Dominions were represented by Prime Ministers. At the end of the last century the Dominions started Imperial Preference and they had continued and developed this.

When we had little industrial competition and expanding markets, free trade was obviously good business, but the rapid development of foreign industry [Plate 1a] and the growth of foreign tariffs changed the position completely. From 1875 to 1890, while our trade with foreign countries remained stagnant, our Empire trade doubled.

The Dominion representatives said that Empire settlement must depend on markets and that, unless they could see a market assured, it was impossible for them to encourage settlement on a large scale and to incur financial commitments entailed by intensive development programmes. The Australian Prime Minister stated emphatically that the continuance of the Murray River Irrigation Scheme must depend on the market which could be afforded by the preference on dried and canned fruits.

The British Government agreed to new preferences: (i) the stabilisation of the sugar preference; (ii) increased preferences on a number of articles such as tobacco, wines and dried fruit; (iii) new duties on apples, canned fish, canned and dried fruit which the Empire produce in large quantities, with freedom from duty for Empire products.

It was impossible to give effect to the recommendations before the General Election; and after the election the Conservatives resigned. The Labour Government declined to adopt any of the preferences.

P. C. Lister, *I remember*, 1948.

# Comment

This extract is from the memoirs of Viscount Swinton, who was President of the Board of Trade in the Bonar Law Conservative Government, 1922.

Britain's economic position had been slowly declining. By 1922 the position had become serious.

However, Empire trade was on the increase. The 'White Dominions' had strong ties with Britain and tended to buy British goods where possible. Their ability to buy depended largely on their income from the sales of their agricultural produce. If the home country bought their produce the Empire would then have the money to buy British goods.

Lister thought Imperial Preference a business proposition. Others, e.g. Montagu Norman (Document 4), wanted to maintain Free Trade and opposed tariffs. Others, e.g. the Labour Party, saw tariffs as increasing prices here, and so lowering the standard of living.

# Questions

a. What was Imperial Preference?
b. '. . . a practical business proposition'. How does your answer to Question (e) in Document 38 agree with this?
c. When was Free Trade 'good business'? Why?
d. Why had the position changed (Documents 2, 37 and 38)?
e. Why was Australia anxious to find 'a market assured' for 'canned and dried fruits'?
f. How did the Government propose to help the Empire countries?
g. Why were these proposals not adopted?
h. What evidence is there that the Dominions bought British goods? Why was it natural for them to buy manufactured goods from Britain?

# 40 The End of Free Trade

On February 4th, 1932, 'the great day of my life', the House and galleries were full. He took the notes from the red dispatch box which had been his father's as Colonial Secretary. A general tariff, he claimed, would help to correct the balance of payments, raise fresh revenue, and decrease unemployment by transferring 'to our own factories work which is now done elsewhere'. He therefore moved that there should be charged on all goods imported save those specifically exempted, a duty of 10 per cent of their value. By this the Government hoped to encourage home industry and to secure a bargaining factor in tariff negotiations with other countries. None of the new duties would apply to goods from the Dominions.

Then, he came to the peroration —

'There can have been few occasions when to the son has been vouchsafed the privilege of setting the seal on the work which the father began. Nearly 29 years have passed since the great campaign in favour of Imperial Preference. More than 17 years have gone by since he died, convinced that, in some form, his vision would eventually take shape. His work was not in vain. Time and the misfortunes of the country have brought conviction to many. I believe he would have found consolation for the bitterness of his disappointment if he could have foreseen that these proposals would be laid before the House of Commons in the presence of one and by the lips of the other of his sons.'

Austen came down and silently shook hands with his brother while the House cheered and cheered again.

Iain Macleod, *Neville Chamberlain*, 1961.

# Comment

This is an extract from the biography of Neville Chamberlain. He had become Chancellor of the Exchequer in the Coalition Government in 1931 (see Document 43). The Cabinet of ten was made up of four Labour, four Conservative and two Liberal members. The majority of the Cabinet were opposed to tariffs, and yet, as the extract shows, it allowed Chamberlain to introduce a general tariff.

Neville Chamberlain was the son of Joseph Chamberlain, who had campaigned for Tariff Reform at the beginning of this century (Documents 2 and 38). He explains the reasons why such tariffs have to be imposed, and points out that support had grown. Unemployment had become a problem in the 1920s (Document 39), and by 1931 there were over 3 million unemployed. The need for some action seemed obvious.

# Questions

*a.* Why did Neville Chamberlain call this 'the great day of my life'?
*b.* What three reasons does he give for a general tariff?
*c.* What tariffs did he propose? How did he intend to use them?
*d.* Why would Dominion goods be cheaper than comparable foreign goods?
*e.* Why had many who did not feel they could agree with Joseph Chamberlain in 1905 support Neville Chamberlain in 1932?
*f.* How does Document 38 show that 'work is now done elsewhere'?
*g.* In what sense does 4th February 1932 mark the end of 19th-century economic history (Document 4 also)?
*h.* Write a paragraph on Imperial Preference. (Tariffs on foreign goods; lower tariffs on Empire products; lower tariffs on British export to Empire countries; gains to Britain and Empire.)

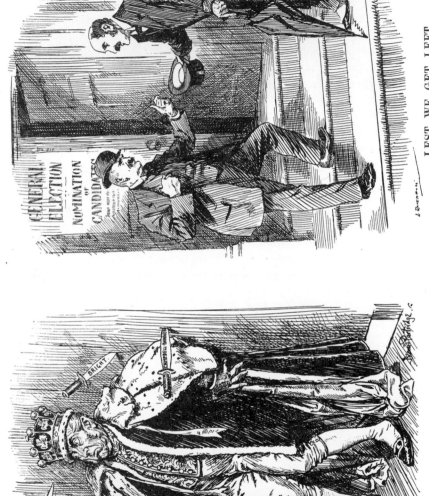

## NERVOUS WORK.

Peer (loq.) "WELL, I SUPPOSE THEY'LL GO ON MISSING ME AS USUAL; BUT I MUST SAY IT'S GETTING RATHER WARM!"

11a.

## LEST WE GET LEFT.

Liberal Candidate. "ON THE DISTINCT UNDERSTANDING THAT THIS IS NOT TO BE REGARDED AS A SIGN OF LASTING AFFECTION, I AM PREPARED, IN THE FACE OF THE COMMON FOE, TO GIVE WAY TO YOU."

Labour Candidate. "SAME HERE."

11b.

# Comment

The Labour Party grew slowly in the first years of the 20th century. In many ways its aims were the same as those of the New Liberalism of Lloyd George (Document 33): both parties co-operated on Workers' Compensation, the introduction of legislation against sweated industries (Document 17) and increased state activity (Document 33).

The Tory Party had been strengthened after 1886 when many former Liberals (the Liberal Unionists) joined the Tory Party. As the Liberal Party became more radical (to try and win the new working-class voters), many former Liberals joined the Tory Party. In particular most of the former Liberal Peers joined the Tories; this made the House of Lords a predominantly Tory House. There were many clashes with the Lords and the Commons. This came to a head in 1909 when the Lords rejected the 'People's Budget' introduced by Lloyd George. This led to the passing of the Parliament Act, 1911, which curtailed the powers of the Lords.

# Questions

a. Against whom are the Liberal and Labour Parties uniting? What evidence is there that they are seeking their own interests?
b. Who attacked the House of Lords?
c. To which political parties do the attackers belong?
d. Why should the Taff Vale decision (Document 30) have made the Labour Party attack the Lords?
e. What is meant by 'they are getting warmer'? When was the power of the House of Lords cut down?

# 41 The Origins of the Parliamentary Labour Party

Before the London Dock Strike (1889) the Trade Union organisation was limited by the high contributions and special qualifications required from its members to little more than half a million; even so, it was richer, more numerous, better officered with men of ability and experience, and more powerful and responsible for the condition of the Labour movement than any other body in the country. Since that time the great unions have adopted new arrangements; practically every wage earner (can) belong to the union of his trade. The establishment of a great number of unions in formerly unorganised trades has trebled the numbers, increased the political power and responsibility of the Trade Union organisation.

Attempts have been made by Socialists to establish societies to relieve the unions of their political duty; at a General Election the union could put up 2,000 voters for every single voter of the most successful of their rivals.

The money difficulty does not exist for unions. A penny a week from every member of a trade union would produce £300,000. This shows how easily the larger unions alone could provide £30,000 to finance 50 Labour candidates at £600 apiece.

Representation of the working classes at the General Election will depend on the trade unions, not on the Socialist bodies. The Fabian Society, the Social Democratic Federation, the Labour Electoral Association and the Independent Labour Party have not the slightest prospect of mustering enough money. Their part will be to provide the agitation which will enable the trade union leaders to obtain the support of the rank and file.

George Bernard Shaw, *Fortnightly Review*, 1st November 1893.

# Comment

Some of the working classes had been given the vote by the Reform Acts of 1867 and 1884 (page 113). For many years after these Acts, working-class members were elected as Liberals ('Lib-Labs'). Thomas Burt (Book I, Document 31) was one of the first of these.

Various Socialist bodies had been formed during the 1880s; these also thought that their best policy would be to convert the Liberal Party to their way of thinking.

By the middle of the 1890s it was clear that this policy had failed. The Gladstonian Liberals (elected in 1892) had little to offer the working-class or the middle-class intellectual Socialists. There was need for an independent party representing the working classes.

Among the first to recognise this was the Fabian Society. This was a middle-class intellectual society; its members included the Webbs (Document 30), Charles Booth and Bernard Shaw, the author of this extract.

# Questions

a. What 'agency' did Shaw think was fit for 'political work?'
b. What brought 'New Unionism before the public'? Why was it called 'new'? (See Document 29.)
c. What five reasons does Shaw give to explain the power of the trade union movement before 1889?
d. How had trade unionism changed since 1889? How had these changes affected the political power of the union movement?
e. How many Socialist organisations are named? What attempts had they made? How did their numbers compare with the members in the trade union movement?
f. How could the unions raise £300,000? Why would each Labour candidate require £600?
g. What part would the Socialist societies play in the working-class party?
h. When was: (i) the first Independent Labour Party member elected to Parliament; (ii) the Parliamentary Labour Party formed; and (iii) when were Members of Parliament first paid a salary?

# 42 Votes for Women and Many Men

1.  (i) A man shall be a parliamentary elector if he is of full age and has residence or business premises qualifications.
    (ii) He must during the whole of the qualifying period have resided in or occupied business premises in the constituency.
    (iii) Business premises means land or other premises occupied for the purpose of business, profession or trade.
2.  A man shall be a parliamentary elector for a university constituency if he is of full age and has received a degree at any university forming part of the constituency.
4.  (i) A woman shall be a parliamentary elector if she has attained the age of thirty years.
8.  A man shall not vote at a general election for more than one constituency for which he is registered by residence, or for more than one constituency for which he is registered by other qualifications.
11. (i) Two registers of electors for each constituency shall be prepared every year; one (the spring register) for the qualifying period ending on the fifteenth of January, the other (the autumn register) for the qualifying period ending on the fifteenth of July.
    (ii) The spring register shall come into force on the fifteenth of April; autumn register shall come into force on the fifteenth of October.
21. At a general election all polls shall be held on one day.
26. A candidate shall deposit with the returning officer the sum of £150.
27. If the number of votes polled by the candidate does not exceed one-eighth of the total number of votes polled the amount deposited shall be forfeited; but in any other case that amount shall be returned to the candidate.

Representation of the People Act, 1918.

# Comment

The Reform Acts of 1867 (Book I, Plate 11) and 1884 had not been completely democratic. Only three men out of every five, and no women, were given the vote. Many men could vote in a number of constituencies where they owned property.

The demand for 'votes for women' had been made as early as 1850; a number of women's organisations took up the cry at the end of the 19th century, some using militant methods, others depending on argument alone.

During the First World War (1914–18) the Government appointed a Conference to examine the question of the franchise. The Act of 1918 was based on the recommendations of this Conference.

By this Act 13 million men and 8.5 million women were entitled to vote, compared with the 7 million men who had been entitled to vote in 1914.

The Act contained a list of constituency changes; each constituency would now contain about 70,000 voters.


# Questions

*a.* How did a man qualify for an ordinary vote?

*b.* When did a man have a business vote?

*c.* What was meant by the qualifying period? Why would some people not have a vote in a General Election?

*d.* At what age could (i) a man, (ii) a woman first qualify for a vote?

*e.* How much money did a candidate have to deposit? Why would this stop some people becoming candidates?

*f.* How many votes could a university-trained business man have at election time?

*g.* When did a candidate lose his deposit?

*h.* When did women gain the vote on equal terms with men?

# 43 The 1931 Political Crisis, 1931

From Thursday, 20th August to Sunday, 23rd August, Mr. Mac-Donald and I had frequent interviews with the Opposition. They maintained that if the Government could not (make more) economies, they would unite and defeat the Government. They were dissatisfied with the proposals for reducing the cost of unemployment payments.

It was decided that (we) should submit to the Opposition that if we could increase the economies by £20,000,000 (£12,500,000 from the Unemployment Grants and £7,500,000 from other sources) they would regard it as satisfactory. We received the impression that they would regard it as satisfactory. They urged that the bankers should be consulted.

We put before the bankers that total economies might be increased by £20,000,000 from the £56,000,000 previously accepted. They thought that this might satisfy New York and the credits sought would be granted.

The split in the Labour Cabinet took place on the proposal to reduce unemployment pay by 10%. The May Committee had recommended a cut of 20%. After a 10% cut in unemployment pay, the recipients of these payments would still be in a better position than they were in 1924. There had been a fall in the cost of living which was equivalent to a 30% increase in the purchasing power of the benefits.

The Cabinet would not agree to implement the authority they had given us to submit suggestions to the Opposition leaders and the bankers. A small majority were in favour of these economies, but, as half the Cabinet would have resigned, the break-up of the Labour Government was inevitable.

Viscount Snowden, *An Autobiography*, 1934.

# Comment

This is an extract from the autobiography of Philip Snowden, a member of the first Labour Government, 1924, and Chancellor of the Exchequer in the second Labour Government, 1929–31.

Both these Labour Governments were minority Governments. They depended on the support of the Liberals.

Under the influence of Montagu Norman (Document 4) the City of London had again become one of the world's leading financial centres. Loans were made to foreign countries and companies, British capital flowed overseas as it had done in the late 19th century (Document 37).

The Bank of England was often forced to borrow money from some countries to lend to others. The Wall Street crash made financiers very wary about their lending; some of them did not approve of the British Government's financial policy up to 1931. They took their money out of Britain (paragraph 3). If this were allowed to continue Britain would cease to be the world's financial centre (Document 4).

# Questions

a. What evidence is there that the Labour Government was a minority Government?
b. What evidence is there that Britain was borrowing from foreign bankers?
c. What did they want the Government to do?
d. How could increased economies be made?
e. Snowden claimed that the unemployed would be better off after the cuts than they had been in 1924. Why was this so?
f. Read Document 34, paragraph 1, again. How would a reduction in unemployment benefit lead to further unemployment?
g. Why did the Government 'break up'?
h. What Government followed the Labour Government of 1929–31?

# 44 Stanley Baldwin

Certainly Mr. Baldwin has possessed an intuitive[1] intelligence, highly developed, and without this, as so many political teachers have said, you may have the politician but not the statesmen. It led him to believe that for this country a conflict of the two extremes of Left and Right could be avoided if his own party, the strongest in the State and embracing the Right, would have the wisdom and courage to shift to the centre ground of a liberalised Toryism. A Nonconformist divine congratulated him on one of his recent emollient[2] speeches on industrial relations. 'Well,' answered Mr. Baldwin, 'I am opposed to Socialism, but I have always endeavoured to make the Conservative Party face left in its anti-Socialism.'

Several things bear testimony to his remarkable success in that aim. One is the relative impotence of the Liberal Party. Another is that he has been the greatest power in the State for fourteen years and has won, or been the chief instrument in winning, three general elections and three great majorities, sweeping into them masses of Liberal and progressive and unattached voters. But it can probably never be done again. The conjunction of his qualities is never likely to be found in another Tory leader — sagacity,[3] subtlety, a temperate mind and a strong dislike of mere partisanship — in short, Burke's average, decent Englishman exalted.

He was the born champion of the middle way given to England at a time when, history may pronounce, she most needed it. He has got the Tory Party to pass Liberal measures entirely repugnant to its ideas. He has never said a wounding word of an opponent.

[1] intuition: knowing the right thing to do.
[2] emollient: calming, soothing, relaxing.
[3] sagacity: wisdom.

H. Boardman, *The Glory of Parliament*, 1960.

11c. Young working men congratulate Mr. Baldwin, May 1923.

## Comment

Stanley Baldwin was Prime Minister in 1923 (Document 39) and 1925 (Document 32). He was the dominant figure in the Coalition formed by MacDonald in 1931, and succeeded MacDonald in 1935.

One of the reasons why Britain did not go through the Fascist/Communist struggle was the policy of Baldwin. This extract is from the memoirs of Harry Boardman, for many years the Parliamentary Correspondent of the *Manchester Guardian*. He is writing about the value of the work done by Baldwin.

## Questions

*a.* What is meant by 'extremes of left and right'?
*b.* How, according to Baldwin, could a conflict between left and right be avoided?
*c.* What had he 'always endeavoured to make the Conservative Party' do?
*d.* Read Document 15 again. What 'Liberal measures' are mentioned there?
*e.* Give three proofs of Baldwin's 'remarkable success'.
*f.* What had happened to the Liberal Party?
*g.* For whom were former Liberals now voting?
*h.* Give the dates of the three General Elections which Baldwin had won.

# Comment

These plates illustrate the rise in the living standards of working-class people in East London after 1894. In part this was due to legislation (Documents 14, 15 and 27), in part to falling prices (Document 1) and in part to education. The children in Plate 12a grew up to become the parents of children in Plate 12b, who in turn became the parents of the children in Plate 12c. (See also Plates 4a and 4b again.)

# Questions

a. How does the quality of clothing indicate improved living standards for children of this area?
b. Which children look healthiest? Why do you think so?
c. Many children in Plate 12c have glasses. How many of the children in the other plates wear glasses? Can you suggest one reason for this?
d. Which group of children do you think would have the best chance of doing well at school? Why?
e. Imagine a conversation between a child from Plates 12a and c. What would they have to say about: (i) school meals; (ii) secondary schools; (iii) medical inspection?

12. The social revolution: a group from the same school taken in 1894 (a), 1924 (b), and 1957 (c).

# 45 The Workpeople's Polytechnic

The demand for higher education is heard on all sides. It is taken up by Parliament; the London County Council are devoting large sums to it. One experiment is the Polytechnic Institute in Regent Street; it owes its existence to the energy, and munificence, of Mr. Quintin Hogg . . . The classes are of two kinds, science and art classes; and industrial classes, which are related to the City and Guilds of London Institute of Technical Instruction. Industrial classes are subdivided into classes of mechanics and into 'practical trade classes' for apprentices and young workmen . . . The wonder is that young men spend the evening in doing the work that they have been employed upon all day; but such is the case; the class-rooms are filled. These (lads) are led partly by the desire of learning, and partly by the wish to better themselves; for example, a young plasterer comes, learns his lesson, perhaps emigrates to America, finds himself able to earn four times the wages of a single plasterer in London. In the engineering room, young men may be seen interesting themselves in the joining of a screw; the room is full of lathes and other small machines, made and finished by the boys . . .

The need for higher education is every day becoming more present to the public. Our commercial prosperity is being threatened by competition all over the world; it will be impossible for us to keep our markets unless our workmen are on a level with the best workmen in Paris, Berlin or Philadelphia.

*The Times*, quoted by Ethel M. Hogg, *Quintin Hogg — a biography*, 1904.

## Comment

The Forster Education Act, 1870, had dealt with primary education for all up to the age of 11 (Book I, Document 48). Further education was provided by the public schools, the local grammar schools and some charity schools. The State took no part.

12d. The Regent Street Polytechnic. The portrait is of Quintin Hogg, the founder.

The demand was met first by private philanthropy. Quintin Hogg spent £100,000 of his own money on the founding of the Regent Street Polytechnic.

# Questions

a. What evidence is there that an interest in higher education was being taken by: (i) the State; (ii) local authorities; (iii) workpeople?
b. Who founded the Polytechnic in Regent Street? Why?
c. What kind of classes were held there?
d. Who went to the industrial classes?
e. What were the advantages to the students: (i) as craftsmen; (ii) as wage-earners?
f. What evidence is there that foreign competition was affecting British industry?
g. What evidence is there that foreign countries provided better qualified workmen than did Britain? What were the effects of this?
h. Why did the newer industries require more educated workpeople? (See Documents 3, 5, 9 and 47.)

# 46 The Education Act, 1902

You have given to County and Borough Councils the right to intervene in respect of technical instruction alone; the normal growth of secondary education has been warped. Higher technical instruction can . . . only do its work well when (it) is based on a sound general secondary education.

I (do) not blame the School Boards because they have trespassed on the territories of secondary education . . . But . . . these authorities have exaggerated their capacity for dealing with . . . secondary education . . . no mere addition of higher classes at the top of the elementary schools will carry out the objects we have in view . . .

Our reform must establish one authority for education — technical, secondary, primary — possessed of power, to provide for the training of teachers, and for the welding of higher technical and higher secondary education on to the University system. . . . This authority, responsible for a heavy cost to the rate payers, should be the rating authority of the district.

A vast expenditure of public money has yet left this country behind all its Continental and American rivals. A huge average cost per child in our elementary schools (leaves) many of these schools half starved, inadequately equipped, imperfectly staffed. A development of University life by private liberality which has no parallel except in America has covered our great industrial centres with Universities where the very highest type of University instruction is given. (Our) technological institutions I am afraid do not yet rival those which America and Germany have produced, but within their limits are admirable . . . Yet these Colleges and institutions never will effect all they might do so long as our secondary education, which is their necessary preparation, is in the imperfect condition in which we find it . . .

Speech by A. J. Balfour, Prime Minister, introducing the Bill in the House of Commons, 24th March 1902.

# Comment

County Councils and County Boroughs had been created in 1888 as administrative bodies.

These new Councils had been given the power to provide technical schools for their areas. The state primary schools remained with the School Board (Book I, Document 48). Some of these Boards had started classes for older pupils who wished to stay at school after the age of 11. In these 'higher' or 'senior' classes the Board taught science, art and technical subjects.

The Board of Education had been set up in 1899 and Robert Morant was its chief Civil Servant. He was regarded as one of the most outstanding examples of the new type of Civil Servant (Documents 18 and 27). He was anxious to create an orderly educational system with a Board which would act through the County Councils to provide both primary and secondary education.

# Questions

a. Name three authorities mentioned in the extract.
b. What schools were provided by the County Councils?
c. What schools were provided by the local School Boards?
d. Some School Boards had opened classes for technical and higher education. What did Balfour think of this development?
e. What powers did Balfour want 'one authority for education' to have?
f. What evidence is there that Britain was still behind foreign countries in: (i) primary education; (ii) technology?
g. Why was an extension of secondary education required in 1902? (See also Documents 2, 3, 5 and 47.)
h. Why was a reform in education administration required at this time?

# 47 Britain's Lack of Scientists

We suffer from want of experts. Instead of experts being diffused, as they are in Switzerland, in the United States, we have taken too few steps to produce experts. It is no use saying to the manufacturers, 'Employ more chemists.' There are no chemists. Our training machine is not adequate to produce the supply we require. At the beginning of the war, I found that we had become dependent upon Germany to an alarming degree; in regard even to great discoveries that we had made in this country it had been left to the Germans to produce what we wanted. I asked why and was told, 'We cannot get chemists. The Germans make the produce in such a way that it is best to buy from them.'

The other day I inquired how many chemists there were for the hundreds of chemical industries in this country, because many of the chemical works were without chemists. I found that there were only 1500 trained chemists in this country altogether. Our public schools do not aim at preparing boys' minds for the study of chemistry; nor do our secondary schools; nor have we any trade continuation schools which stimulate the working man's son. Nor are our Universities equipped to produce these men in large numbers. We have only 1500 trained chemists in this country. On the other hand four large German chemical firms, which have played havoc with certain departments of our trade, employ 1000 highly trained chemists between them, trained and produced by the great schools which exist there.

In this country we have the very highest science and knowledge, but we have not enough individuals possessing that high science and knowledge to go round. The result is that we suffer . . .

Lord Haldane speaking in the House of Lords, 12th July 1916.

# Comment

This extract is from a speech made by Lord Haldane in the House of Lords in 1916. He gives an account of the shortage of British scientists and of British chemists in particular. In doing so he also touches on the question of education.

A minority of the population was being highly educated at our universities. A minority of people were leaders in the field of science and technology. There were not enough people with this training.

Haldane explains what he thinks are the reasons for this state of affairs. The public schools provided the business leaders and financiers; the grammar schools provided a basic education for the middle ranks.

The Act of 1902 (Document 46) had made some changes, but these had not yet had time to make up for the mistakes of the past.


# Questions

a. What evidence is there of our failure to provide a technical service?
b. How successful had other countries been in this matter?
c. Britain was being overtaken by Germany (see Documents 2 and 3). How does this extract help to explain some reasons for Germany's success?
d. How many trained chemists did Haldane find in Britain?
e. How many had he found in 'four large German chemical firms'?
f. We had too few chemists. How far did Haldane think that (i) public schools, (ii) secondary schools, (iii) technical schools were to blame for this?
g. What evidence is there that British inventions were being taken up in Germany and not in Britain?
h. How would the Balfour Education Act, 1902, help to remedy the deficiencies mentioned by Haldane?

# 48 Secondary Education for All

There is a point at which (all children) ought to begin their post-primary education; it is important to remember that such education will be successful only (if) it is related to the requirements of the children. There are diversities of gifts and there must be diversity of education. Education should not attempt to press different types of character and intelligence into a single mould, but should provide a range of educational opportunity to appeal to varying interests.

What proportion of the children leaving primary schools should pass to such (secondary) schools? It is not possible, we think to say. At present it appears to be approximately 8·3%. It is desirable that it should be largely increased. The growth of secondary education in the last twenty years had been one of the most remarkable movements of our day, and nothing should cramp its future development.

The extension of the name Grammar School to cover the larger number of County and Municipal Secondary Schools founded since 1902 involves a new departure. But the name seems to us to have several advantages. It suggests a curriculum in which languages and literature, also mathematics and natural science, play a considerable part. It links the newer developments to an ancient and dignified tradition for culture.

For the second and third type of school a name is needed. We think that the word 'Modern' expresses adequately what we mean — that the education which these schools offer gives a prominent place to studies whose bearing on practical life is obvious and immediate.

*Board of Education — Report of the Hadow Committee*, 1926.

## Comment

Legislation (1907) following the Balfour Act, 1902, allowed a minority of children to go free at the age of 11 to the old and new grammar schools. The majority of children remained at their elementary school until they reached the school-leaving age.

This is an extract from the Report issued by this Committee under the Chairmanship of Sir William Hadow. The document shows that

12e. Children's trip to Bognor, July 1913.

there were some children (about 8·3%) leaving elementary schools to go to grammar schools. It showed that in some areas only 5% went on to such schools while in other areas as many as 27% did so.

By 1938 63% of children were in separate secondary schools, but many authorities were slow to build new schools. The 1944 Education Act completed the separation of primary from secondary education.

## Questions

a. What is meant by 'post primary education'?
b. What percentage of children went to grammar schools in 1926?
   Why does this extract speak of 'growth in the last 20 years'?
c. Why, according to this Report, should there be a variety of secondary schools?
d. What schools were, in 1926, called grammar schools?
e. What, according to the extract, should be taught in grammar schools?
f. What sort of education should be provided in the other secondary schools? What should these schools be called?
g. What evidence is there that the 1902 Act had had some influence? Was the Hadow Committee satisfied with the progress made?
h. Write a paragraph each on: (i) the Fisher Education Act, 1918; (ii) the Butler Education Act, 1944.

# Conclusion

During the period 1870–1939 Britain lost her place as the world's industrial leader (Section 1); the industries on which that leadership was based, coal and cotton, became less important (Section 2). New countries became industrial leaders; new industries grew; new methods of transport changed the world's economic pattern and British social life (Section 3).

During this period great efforts were made to deal with the social problems created by the earlier Industrial Revolution. Improved housing and welfare provision (Section 4) and improved working conditions (Section 5) were accompanied by improved treatment of the poor (Section 7).

New trade unionism (Section 8) and the rise of the Parliamentary Labour Party (Section 11) were partly responsible for this changed attitude; the changing natures of the Liberal Party (Document 27) and of the Conservative Party (Section 11) were both cause and effect of this change.

As Britain ceased to lead the world, new problems arose. One of these was unemployment, which became a major problem after 1920. Various attempts were made to deal with it (Sections 7 and 10). More important was the development of new ideas on how to deal with this problem. A number of writers began to question the *laissez-faire* ideas of the 19th century; they proposed an increase in state activity (Section 9).

Throughout this period, living standards improved for the majority of the population (Section 6). A greater number of people shared more fully in the wealth of the country, as Graves and Hodge noted (Documents 11 and 24).

In Book III we will see how the ideas put forward in this period (1870–1939) were put into practice. We will also see a continued rise in living standards. One writer has said that Britain in the 1950s was a country with an 'endless middle class' — i.e. there were very few rich people, very few very poor people; the majority of the population had a comfortable living standard. If this is so, the beginnings of this 'endless middle' are to be found in the period covered by the documents which you have studied in Book II.